Someone
We need to
Listen to

Hearing from God: a workbook

By Iain Dunbar

Oxford, UK

Paperback ISBN: 978-1-80031-186-2
Ebook ISBN: 978-1-80031-185-5

www.newgeneration-publishing.com

New Generation Publish

Contents

What people who have read this book are saying...

Iain's workbook provides practical, biblical instruction "to know what your callings in life might be" [xiv] and "to encourage you to explore what the Bible really says about God's habit of speaking to people ... as a normal part of everyday life." [xiii] And the workbook delivers on these promises. But it's more than that. The hidden gem, the onion inside the onion is the foundational basis of his instruction: Pride and being a child.

It's pride that prevents us from hearing God. "the word of God to us must, at some level, be a challenge to 'self [page 79]'". As C. S. Lewis said, "The essential vice, the utmost evil, is Pride." We all know this. We leave little room for God's direction when we are so consumed with "self."

The antidote? Humble, child-like submission. "In order to see and relate to 'the rightful King', you need a child-like nature. [page 2]" "'I am telling you this in solemn truth: he who does not accept the kingdom of God in the way in which a child would, will never find entry into it.'" [page 75]

It's this simplicity that makes Iain's workbook, about the daily discovery of God's voice, so useful. Not a long tick-list of to-dos, but solid instruction for guiding our daily lives.

John Fox – President & Founder, Venture Marketing, Greater Chicago Area

'Someone we need to listen to' is a very useful resource for individuals or small groups wishing to move on from the shallow waters of basic belief to the choppy seas of actually having a two-way conversation with God about what is on his heart for us to do as individuals.

It has the potential to redirect life and bring meaning and fulfilment to our daily work, whether that be paid or voluntary, long or short term. Referring to Old and New Testament stories, and drawing on stories from the lives of others, Iain unpacks examples of how God longs to speak and to make Himself known to his people. The book ends with a challenge to commit to active listening for God's voice in our daily lives.

This is a refreshing approach to the subject of communicating with God, offering practical insights into how we might hear God's voice above life's noise.

Bob Fraser – Regional Director, England (NW), Christian Vision for Men (CVM)

'Someone We need to Listen to', is a powerful and provocative workbook that can stand on its own or be used in a small group (community group) setting. It hits on the challenges we face (or, in some cases, intentionally put in front of ourselves) to effectively hearing God's instructions for our life.

Understanding when God is speaking to us is as challenging sometimes as discerning what He is instructing us to do. But, working through some of the practical steps outlined in this book, learning to listen, and reflecting on scripture will bring you one step closer to understanding how to interpret God's leading.

It is a quick but effective read, which addresses what we have to do to accomplish a real conversation with God.

Rob Corrao – CEO, LAC Group, Los Angeles

The God of the universe is intent on interacting with us every day! Our part is to develop an expectation that He will actually speak. Through this Workbook, Iain has challenged and helped me to think broadly, but practically, about how growing in hearing the voice of God is crucial for:

- My relationship with God – the two-way interaction that is the foundation of all life and work;
- My relationship with myself and others;
- How I understand and execute the assignments God has for me. Acts 13:36 says "David served his generation according to the will of God..." David was a man who had daily interaction with God and asked Him about both strategic and tactical assignments. I long for that sort of experience too. Thank you, Iain for the provocation.

Fellow reader, may you be similarly stirred about the adventure of hearing God and about working with Him in this broken world that He cares for so deeply.

Oliver Nyumbu – Leadership & Strategy Specialist, Birmingham, UK

Looking back God was always there. During both the mundane and the critical decisions, striving to listen to His will has proven both freeing and a lifelong journey. Through Jesus, we have the amazing possibility of speaking and listening to the maker of the Universe, 'Who is Not Silent'.

At a time when distractions are at their peak in a fast-paced world, making time for God has become critical.

Carlos Nunes – Acc Mgt. & Business Devt., Cummins Inc., Northamptonshire, UK

Throughout 'Someone We Need to Listen To', Iain's passion for people to hear God communicating with them is evident on every page. The book has reminded me how God spoke (in scripture) through such a diverse group of people, some of whom were his chosen people and some who were not; some who believed in him and some who did not.

We may impose limitations on Him but God is not limited either in who He speaks to or what He says and a deepening of our relationship with Him will result in a greater capacity to hear his voice in a multitude of ways. I am also comforted that He perseveres with us even though we do not always hear that well.

James Mondon – Engineering Project Manager, Bridgnorth UK

God wants to speak to us through our families, friends, co-workers and mentors. He speaks through His Word, as revealed in the Bible, and through various other media. From my own experience, He has also used those who don't profess any faith, to prod and provoke me to action.

However, I have at times dismissed certain 'imaginations' or 'prompts' as improbable, so I've had to learn over the years how to intentionally seek His voice. I trust that the insights Iain shares in this invaluable book will inspire you (and perhaps even save you a few years!) in your personal journey towards hearing God.

Andrew Marriott – Executive Director, MotiVate (Missionary Ventures), New Zealand

In the past, I felt intimidated when friends appeared to hear from God about life's smallest daily details. When it didn't seem to happen for me, I wondered if God didn't have any opinion as to what I did, so long as I was obedient to the general commands in Scripture.

But I found great encouragement in Jesus' words: if our Father cares enough to feed the birds and the clothe the flowers, then 'how much more' he cares about the specifics of my life. I've found that, through the unfolding of events over the years, through a gentle certainty in my heart, and with specific words in Scripture, he has often given me clear guidance with Fatherly care and patience.

Revd Daniel Hames – Associate Director, Union Foundation, Oxfordshire UK

We often hear God's voice with greater clarity when we have stilled ourselves and yet many of us live busy lives and have stressful jobs. How can I possibly hear God amongst all the distractions of the day? I have found it helpful to take a 'Selah' moment, as described in the Psalms. Take a pause, take a breath, consider Him, and invite Him to speak.

Rarely do we hear an audible voice - more often we have a 'sense', a nudge, a prompting, a thought, a peace, or a change of mind, about something. I believe that when we ask God for direction or inspiration or ask him "What do you think Lord?", we should then pay special attention to the scriptures/thoughts that come to mind and to the feelings we experience afterwards. After all a conversation is two-way, why wouldn't he answer us?

Richard Hooke – Campus Pastor, The Well Church, Lancashire UK

Sometimes I hear the Lord through the Word, sometimes through what someone else says, sometimes through circumstance or through nature, and sometimes thoughts just popping into my head! I remember someone who had walked with the Lord for many years telling me that, when you need to make a big decision in life, it is good to have 3 confirmations – to hear His voice 'Spirit to spirit'; to see something written in the Word; and to hear it from some other, trusted person.

From personal experience, once you have heard the Lord's voice and been obedient, whatever the world / the enemy throws at you, you can confidently stand on the Rock!

Emma Maitland-Carew – Nutritional Therapist, Oxfordshire UK

Sometimes, (and it's not for lack of wanting or trying, I don't think), I've found discerning what God is saying incredibly difficult. It is tempting in those moments to think "well, it can't be that important then" or "maybe He just wants me to get on with whatever I think is best". But the thing is, when you look at Scripture, you can't get away from the fact that God is always talking to the people who love Him (and even to people who don't).

He speaks to give direction and motivation; He speaks to effect change; He speaks to share His own heart and to enter into friendship with people. I'm discovering that it's worth persisting through the (not insubstantial) challenges and it's worth taking the help and encouragement offered in this book, because His voice is the only genuine source of confidence and comfort that I've ever found.

Joy Cowley – Projects & Implementation Lead, TLG, Yorkshire UK

Introduction

Francis Schaeffer was a theologian and philosopher who wrote a series of books both defending and articulating the truth of the Christian Faith. One of them was called 'He is There and He is not Silent' and, over the years, that has become one of my favourite statements. However, although learning to communicate more effectively with God is very important to me, I would be the last to claim that it is easy.

Communication between us and God obviously does not happen via a voice call or a text message or an email, or the like. It is a 'spirit to spirit' thing.

When Jesus was in Samaria, talking to the woman at the well, He spoke of the normality of 'spirit to spirit' communication by saying, 'Woman, believe me, the hour is coming when neither on this mountain nor in Jerusalem will you worship the Father... the hour is coming, and is now here, when true worshipers will worship the Father *in spirit and truth*, for the Father is seeking such people to worship Him. God is spirit, and those who worship Him must worship in spirit and truth' John 4:21-24.

In the Greek text, when Jesus says 'God is spirit', not only is there no article (e.g. an 'a' or a 'the') before the word 'spirit' but also the word occurs first in the sentence. So, Jesus, sounding a bit like Yoda in Star Wars, is actually saying, 'Spirit is God in His very essence'! The word 'spirit' also means 'breath' and so God, in Himself, is the very evidence of life and hence is known, in many places, as 'The Living God'.

As to the agency by whom communication between us and God is supposed to work, Jesus told the disciples that His Father would send someone called 'the Spirit of truth' or 'the Holy Spirit', 'whom the world cannot receive, because it neither sees him nor knows him. (But) You know him, for he dwells with you and will be in you' John 14:16,17. Then Paul, when he is talking about us being accepted into God's family and about the work of the Holy Spirit, says, 'For all who are led by the Spirit of God are sons of God... you have received the Spirit of adoption as sons, by whom we cry, "Abba! Father!" The Spirit himself bears witness with our spirit that we are children of God' Romans 8:14-16.

God's intention seems clear – He wants to be with us, to dwell in us, to lead us and for us to know Him. As Jesus said in John 14:23, 'If anyone loves me, he will keep my word, and my Father will love him, and we will come and make our home with him.'

So, if that's the case and the person we are hearing from is not so much 'external' as 'internal' – His Spirit bearing witness with or communing with our spirit – then receiving a message or coming to know something will probably be more like 'sensing' than 'hearing'. We might also describe it as getting an impression of something or knowing that we know something which we didn't know before.

To take this train of thought a step or two further... whenever we hear or sense God saying something; whenever we acquire insight or truth; whenever God catches our attention by some means, He is imparting information to us but it is actually more than that. By the very nature of His word, He is also communicating something of *Himself*. His word is living truth and it is always actively working – in every word He speaks, He is conveying something of His very essence.

God's intention is always to be creative and to establish something tangible by means of His word – He spoke the world into existence, as recorded in Genesis 1 and 2, and the first few verses of John's gospel tell us that His Word, present 'by His side' at the very beginning, was a some*one* rather than a some*thing*. The Word had a big 'W' and it was through this some*one* that everything came into being.

To put it another way; when John 1:3,4 says, 'All things came into being through *him*, and there was nothing that came into being apart from *him*. In *him* there was life, that life which was ever the light of men...' (Cassirer, 1989), it is stating (among other things) that, right from the beginning, God was establishing the foundational principle of communication with His creation – namely, that He imparts not just words but His own Word.

As chronicled in the Old Testament, God revealed Himself to mankind and took for Himself a nation, through whom He demonstrated how righteousness was supposed to become established, both individually and corporately, but this was just a shadow of what was to come. He knew the seriousness of our plight as wayward and sinful people and so, instead of words being written on stone tablets,

He intended that those words somehow be written into our hearts.

A different kind of Word was necessary which, when 'spoken', would provide His presence here among us – a living model of what life and relationship and daily interaction with a creator was always meant to look like. This was the Father's ultimate piece of communication, described by John as follows: 'So the Word became a creature of flesh and blood and made his stay in our midst. And we saw His glory, the glory which is his as the Father's only Son, coming forth from the Father, full of grace and truth.' John 1:14 (Cassirer, 1989)

The incarnation of Jesus is the indelible proof of God's abiding principle of communication. As Hebrews 1:1-3 says, 'Long ago, … God spoke to our fathers by the prophets, but in these last days he has spoken to us by his Son, …through whom also He created the world. He (the Son) …upholds (or continues to sustain) the universe by the word of his power.' Everything we know and everything we see around us is all about God speaking to us in Jesus. Our only way forward – the only option we have for life and breath – is to learn to receive His Word and it is meant to be a glorious experience; a daily dialogue by which we progressively appreciate His grace and truth.

Unfortunately, there is not as much practical teaching in our churches, encouraging individuals to hear God for themselves, as there should be. Neither are there enough accessible materials, describing the principles of daily communication with God, as there should be. Hence, my desire to create a resource that sets out, as systematically as possible, some of the principles of 'hearing God'.

So, how should you use this resource? There is necessarily some teaching material here but the objective is less about teaching and more about storytelling – relating how God captured the attention of people throughout Bible-times and then delivered messages to them. It is also about giving you opportunities to reflect on your own experience and expectations. The Q&A sections are intended to facilitate that reflection.

The main purpose of the workbook is to encourage you to explore what the Bible *really* says about God's habit of speaking to people and for that to build your expectation of hearing Him as a normal part of everyday life. It may seem that I'm both advocating and expecting a constant dialogue with God, with us hearing Him about every element of our daily lives, including what we have for breakfast, but that's not the case. I'm really trying to redress the balance, given that most of us either tend not to ask Him about very much at all or if we do, expect very little in terms of response.

What does scripture indicate our realistic expectation should be? Jesus' parable of the sheep and the shepherd, in John 10, suggests that hearing His voice is (or should be) a 'normal' occurrence. He says, 'I am the good shepherd. I know my own and my own know me... and they will listen to my voice' (verses 14-16). It is about 'knowing' Him – the more we listen to Him the better we will get to know Him and the better we know Him the more easily we will be able to distinguish His voice from other voices. Thus, it behoves us to cultivate the habit of listening, not with a view to unbalanced fanaticism but rather to natural communication with our Father, our Brother, our Head, our Friend and our Helper.

My other purpose in writing on the subject of 'Hearing God' is to provide accompaniment to the book 'Something for You to Do', which seeks to give a biblical perspective on 'Calling', 'Craftsmanship' and 'Finding your Element'. In order to know what your callings in life might be, in fact to get any understanding of what God might be giving you to do (be it short term projects or long-term vocation), you will need to be able to hear what He is saying to you. Hence this attempt to provide some instruction.

References Used

Biblical quotes/references are taken from the English Standard Version (ESV) or the New King James Version (NKJV), unless indicated otherwise:

- Scripture quotations from the ESV® Bible (The Holy Bible, English Standard Version®), copyright © 2001 by Crossway, a publishing ministry of Good News Publishers. Used by Permission. All rights reserved.
- Scripture quotations from the New King James Version. Copyright © 1982 by Thomas Nelson, Inc. Used by permission. All rights reserved.

I also use a translation of the New Testament by a Jewish professor of philosophy called Heinz Cassirer (Cassirer, 1989). He was a classics scholar, who taught at Glasgow University and Oxford (Corpus Christi) and accepted Jesus as Messiah relatively late in life, having determined to read both Old and New Testaments. He then set out to translate the New Testament and to apply a Jewish lens to the way it is expressed, with the result that his translation is both scholarly and refreshing.

Hearing God requires a changed nature and new building materials

"Jesus spoke to them thus: "...I can give you solemn assurance of this. He who does not accept the kingdom of God in the way in which a child would, will never find entry into it."
Mark 10:15 (Cassirer, 1989)

"Jesus said to them, 'Truly I say to you, the Son can do nothing of His own accord, but only what He sees the Father doing. For whatever the Father does, the Son does likewise.'"
John 5:19

Being a child

The practical truth of our fallen existence is that being able to 'hear', or 'sense' or 'see' 'in the Spirit' does not come naturally and none of us has got it all right – we are all prone to error, presumption and imbalance. Indeed, what Paul said to the Corinthians is just as true today as it was then – 'For now we see in a mirror dimly, but then face to face. Now I know in part; then I shall know fully, even as I have been fully known.' 1Corinthians 13:12.

There is a scene near the beginning of *Prince Caspian* – part of the Chronicles of Narnia, by C. S. Lewis – where Lucy, the youngest of the family, sees the shadow of the great lion, Aslan, moving in a certain direction to 'lead' them in the way they should go. This is the second time the children have been summoned to Narnia and already there is more than a hint that, in order to see and relate to 'the rightful King', you need a child-like nature.

When Lucy relates what she has seen, nobody really believes her. Although the next oldest, Edmund, votes to follow her suggested path, the consensus among both humans and Narnian creatures is that Lucy has imagined the whole thing and they all end up travelling in the opposite direction, with near disastrous consequences.

If you choose to tackle the material in this workbook, be it personally or in a small group, my prayer is that it will equip you to 'see' a little better and to 'hear' a little more clearly and thus be more confident to follow the rightful King in the right direction.

For those of us who have no history of hearing what God is saying; no examples or anecdotes that come to mind of times when we know He clearly directed us, we must come aside and urgently and earnestly petition Him to mentor us in the art of hearing. Ask Him firstly to point out where and how our sight has become veiled and our hearing dulled and then that He would graciously teach us how to distinguish His voice from the other voices and the background noise.

For those who have a bit of a track record of listening and hearing but know there is a great deal more 'land to be possessed', successfully appreciating what God is saying does not require us to lay down our intellect and powers of reason in order to promote spiritual receptivity. However, depending on how we employ those powers, they can inhibit or distort our hearing. It may require the Holy Spirit to dust off our spiritual antennae and to clear the channels and one of the things we definitely need to ask Him for, if we are to become His children and to develop into the fulness of 'sonship', is a child-like nature.

If we don't learn to come to Him like a child to his/her father, we will too easily forget that His ways are not the same as our ways and we'll tend to filter what He is saying through our own experience of the world, our own likes and dislikes and (worst of all) our own fears, phobias, hurts and neuroses. All of which might drastically alter our perception of what He is trying to say or perhaps block it altogether.

Building a wall

Let's attempt an analogy at this point and hope it paints a helpful picture – walking with God on a daily basis, interacting with Him and following His promptings is a little bit like building a dry-stone wall, as opposed to building a wall out of bricks and mortar.

Most of us know what building with bricks and mortar looks like, even if we haven't tried it. If you *have* tried it, you'll know that it's more difficult than it looks but most people can get the hang of it, after a while. As long as the mortar is of the right consistency and you use roughly the right amount on each brick, the result will look like a wall. In fact, it will look like almost every other wall made of bricks and mortar.

The reason it doesn't take a long time to work out how to make progress is that every brick you pick up is exactly the same size and shape as the previous one and lining them up properly can be achieved with a taut piece of string, a spirit level and, from time to time, a plumb line. An experienced bricklayer makes rapid progress mostly 'by eye' and occasional use of the spirit level.

However, building a dry-stone wall is a different science altogether. There are a few important principles to adhere to but there is no mortar to stick stones to other stones and every stone you pick up is different in size, weight and shape to the previous one.

You cannot apply a formula or think several steps ahead when dry-stone walling and you have to consider the position and orientation of each individual component. I trust you can see what I'm trying to get at – life with God is not meant to conform to a recognisable shape and pattern and, as the disciples found when following Jesus, He rarely does things in precisely the same way twice.

We will be looking at lots of examples both of God communicating remotely with people and of Jesus communicating directly with people when He walked the earth. What we'll discover is that, just as Jesus was always alert to what the Father was doing, He wants us to be 'on our toes' at all times; to be dependent on Him for guidance; to be on the lookout for His preferred outcome at each and every stage; to become used to an organic and interactive way of living 'in the Spirit'; and to derive the satisfaction of achieving something unique and lasting in the process.

I'm told there is also something different about the enjoyment derived from the process of building in this way. If you talk to a dry-stone walling expert, it is clear that they deeply appreciate what they do and they will talk about the mindset they get into when practising their craft. It is normal for them to achieve a rhythm, developing a sort of instinct about which stone to use next and becoming oblivious to wind and rain and other adverse conditions whilst 'in the zone'.

Experienced practitioners eventually manage to adhere to the unwritten rule that you should only ever pick up each stone once – i.e. you 'see' the next one that is needed and will always find an appropriate place for it, if it's the 'right' one.

My friend, Andrew, a Baptist Minister, recently found himself acting as mate to a dry-stone walling expert, who had come to repair part of their chapel in Cumbria. It was raining but Andrew testifies that, even as a novice, sorting, picking and handing stones to the builder, he worked for several hours without noticing the cold or the blood on his hands or the fact that he was soaked. He talks with warmth about the experience and says, even weeks afterwards, he found himself stopping from time to time to look at the piece of wall that he helped to construct.

If you have already decided to follow Jesus and your desire is to get closer to Him and know Him better, studying the ways in which God speaks will open the channels of communication between you and Him wider and the Holy Spirit will lead you into more truth.

If you have not yet decided to follow Jesus, the material here will hopefully make you more curious about a God who is committed to speaking with His children on a regular basis. If, as a result, you begin to hear Him and you agree that He is worth following, I cannot ask for a better outcome – please feel free to use the contact details on the cover of this workbook if you would appreciate some more information or assistance.

God wants to speak to those who 'believe' and to those who do not

"After this Jesus went out and saw a tax collector named Levi, sitting at the tax booth. And He said to him, 'Follow me'. And leaving everything, he rose and followed him. And Levi made him a great feast in his house, and there was a large company of tax collectors and others reclining at table with them. And the Pharisees and their scribes grumbled at Jesus' disciples, saying, 'Why do you eat and drink with tax collectors and sinners?' And Jesus answered them, 'Those who are well have no need of a physician, but those who are sick. I have not come to call the righteous but sinners to repentance.'"
Luke 5:27-32

It is not possible to read the Bible without concluding that God is a persistent communicator. As was stated in the Introduction, Genesis begins with God speaking the world into existence – something that is known as 'divine fiat'. In other words, God only had to utter the words in order to make it happen. The first chapter repeatedly states, 'And God said... and there was...'

Then, having created the heavens and the earth, and man within it, the narrative continues with Him habitually walking and talking with Adam in the world He has made.

The Bible ends with God giving a detailed Revelation to the Apostle John, in which He tells him about the end of all things; and the first chapters of the Revelation have Jesus writing a personal letter to each of seven churches.

The evidence of the biblical record shows that God's habit of speaking to His creation is both relentless in frequency and magnificent in scope. At all points between the beginning and the end He initiates conversation with individuals – with kings, with nobles, with the prophets, with ordinary working men and women, with the faithful and the disobedient, with children, with slaves, with the sick, with the poor.

God typically communicates with us in order to reveal the truth about Himself and His plans for mankind; to convict us of sin and to lead us through repentance to a closer relationship with Him; to give comfort and reassurance as we face a variety of difficulties; to give instructions about what He wants us to do; or to provide wisdom concerning the people and situations that require our help and attention.

At no point will these messages contradict His character or run counter to the truth of His written word. However, they might present challenges for us around what we had assumed Him to be like or how we might have preferred to interpret a particular passage of scripture.

It may seem more intuitively reasonable for God to converse with those who are seeking Him – those to whom faith is something to be desired – but the biblical record shows that it is entirely in line with God's character for Him a) to pursue the lost and look out for the prodigal and b) to employ, whenever and wherever necessary, those who don't yet know Him to achieve His purposes. Which means that

He also frequently speaks to the 'unbeliever', whether they are aware it is Him or not.

When you think about it, everyone who might today be termed a 'believer' has made choices not to be an 'unbeliever' and there was an occasion when God became known to them for the first time. In 1Samuel 3 the boy Samuel, who went on to become one of Israel's greatest prophets, had been dedicated to God by his mother, Hannah, and was ministering in the temple at Shiloh under the tutelage of Eli the priest. Despite being known by the Lord and spending much of his young life 'in His presence', it says of him, 'Now Samuel did not yet know the Lord [for himself], and the word of the Lord had not yet been revealed to him' (Verse 7).

There then followed a night when God came and stood and called out to him repeatedly and Samuel had to learn the difference between the voice of Eli and the voice of God. Samuel's 'set apartness' must have given him some expectation of 'hearing' the divine voice but all children start life being more naturally receptive to God. As we get older and begin to question everything, that natural receptivity wanes and conscious decisions need to be made not to dismiss Him or to block Him out.

Both the psalmist and Jesus express this truth: Psalm 8:2 states, 'Out of the mouth of babies and infants, you have established strength...' and, in Mark 10:15 Jesus says that everybody 'needs to receive the kingdom of God like a child' or else they will not enter it. To restate what was said above, it appears that, for people of all ages, getting to know Him requires a measure of childlike faith.

The upcoming pages celebrate God's commitment to be known by all who will respond to His overtures. We will not just look for evidence of *who* God speaks to and *what* He speaks about, but we'll also look at *how* He does it, illustrating some of the ingenious and creative ways He uses to attract people's attention.

Q&A: Establishing Comfort Levels

Before reading on and in order to establish a baseline for your own personal experience, please try to write down a few notes in response to the following questions:

1. Do you feel comfortable with the idea of God speaking directly to you? Try and elaborate a little – if yes, how did you arrive at that feeling of comfort and if no, why does the idea make you uncomfortable?

2. Have there been occasions, whether frequent or infrequent, when you have had a sense of knowing something and have believed that it was God who somehow made you aware of it? If so, provide two or three examples.

3. In each of the examples you have recorded, what were you doing at the time? Were you reading, talking to someone, sitting alone and thinking, or doing some other activity? What was it that triggered the sense of you knowing that 'something'. Or, were there certain 'somethings' that developed over a period of time?

God pursues and makes Himself known to people near and far

"The heavens declare the glory of God, and the sky above proclaims His handiwork. Day to day pours forth speech, and night to night reveals knowledge... Their voice goes out through all the earth, and their words to the end of the world."
Psalm 19:1,2,4

"I have stretched out my hands all day long to a rebellious people, who walk... according to their own thoughts"
Isaiah 65:2 (NKJV)

"I will make my holy name known in the midst of my people Israel... then the nations shall know that I am the Lord, the Holy One of Israel."
Ezekiel 39:7

If, in these pages, we were only to relate the dealings of God with those of His chosen people it might lead to the criticism that such folk are not a fair representation of humanity. They could be said to have had an in-built experience of, or affinity to, this God. However, many whose experiences are chronicled in the Bible were not followers of the God of Israel or part of the nation of Israel at the time when He grabbed their attention and revealed something to them. Despite their not knowing Him at the time, they were caught up in fulfilling God's sovereign purpose. Some went on to follow Him and to build relationship with Him and some did not. For example:

In the gospel of Matthew, the Wise Men, whose country was far from Israel and who brought their gifts to Jesus, saw something unusual in the pattern of the stars, investigated carefully and then began a remarkable journey to seek out the King of the Jews. This was at a time when God was 'appearing' unexpectedly to a whole variety of people, to point to the birth of His Son and He was responsible for the message that these men detected in the heavens.

When the star led them directly to the home of Joseph and Mary, we are told that they 'rejoiced greatly'. It is also clear, by the nature of their gifts, that they had unusual insight into who Jesus was. They came and worshipped Him and were not only guided *to* Jesus, but were then guided *from* Him, back home again, having been told in a dream to return by a different route. The experience of following God's leading made a lasting impression on their lives.

In the book of Esther, a pagan king, who ruled the kingdom of the Medes and Persians had a very senior government official who was planning both to hang a certain Jew (who had refused to bow down to him) and, for good measure, to annihilate the entire Jewish people. One night, the king found himself unable to sleep. He did not know that it was the God of the Jews who was keeping him awake and who then directed him to read particular portions of the 'book of memorable deeds'. In the chronicles he found evidence of a plot on his own life that had been thwarted by the very one who was due to be hung. He also discovered that this man's act of loyalty and service had never been rewarded.

The king's resolve to honour the one who had saved his life kicked off an amazing sequence of events, worthy of the best plot architects in Hollywood. At a banquet given by the queen the following evening, the senior official's plans unravelled spectacularly – it was revealed that the queen was herself Jewish and that the person sentenced to hang was in fact her cousin. In a frantic attempt to explain his actions, the government official broke royal protocol and was guilty of assaulting the queen. He was hanged on the very gallows he himself had constructed and, at the request of the queen, the king then repeatedly legislated in favour of the Jewish people.

The foregoing examples illustrate that God has interesting and imaginative ways of communicating truth. In Old Testament times God's truth was conveyed through dreams and visions and sovereign interventions but His more general method was to raise up prophets who were His human messengers and who, for the most part, passed on exactly what He told them. In the New Testament, as we stated previously, God's greatest intervention was to introduce His Son, who came to live among us and to convey to us, by showing and telling, exactly what the Father is like.

When the Son ascended, the Father sent the Holy Spirit to indwell the believers and to speak through them to those who had not yet heard. The words of Hebrews 1:1,2 are worthy of being aired a second time: 'God, who at various times and in various ways spoke in time past to the fathers by the prophets, has in these last days spoken to us by His Son, whom He has appointed heir of all things, through whom He also created the world.'

Whether or not someone can point to having had a specific, conscious encounter with God, the Bible suggests that nobody, in all of creation, will ultimately be able to claim that God has not spoken to them. In the verse quoted at the very beginning of this section, we are told that His word has gone out and His nature has been demonstrated in the things He has made. Then in Romans 1:19,20 it says, 'For what can be known about God is plain to them [i.e. 'unrighteous men' – verse 18], because God has shown it to them. For his invisible attributes, namely, his eternal power and divine nature, have been clearly perceived, ever since the creation of the world, in the things that have been made. So, they are without excuse.'

It seems that God has always had a desire to make himself known to us and is always taking initiative to get a word both to those who are seeking him and to those who wouldn't otherwise give Him the time of day.

God is in the habit of actively pursuing people

In Luke 15, Jesus tells the parable of the Lost Sheep. This is an extremely well-known story that He told at a time 'when the tax collectors and sinners were all drawing near to hear him.' (Verse 1). We began this book with a passage from earlier in Luke's gospel, also focusing on 'tax collectors and sinners', where Jesus calls Levi [also known as Matthew] to be a disciple and you can imagine Him telling this parable, at Levi's house, whilst enjoying a meal with that group.

When He says in verse 4, 'What man of you, having a hundred sheep, if he has lost one of them, does not leave the ninety-nine in the open country, *and go after the one that is lost, until he finds it?*', he is inviting unanimous agreement. And then, in verses 5 & 7, when He describes the man's joyous reaction to finding the sheep, He concludes by saying, 'Just so, I tell you, there will be more joy in heaven over one sinner who repents than over ninety-nine righteous persons who need no repentance'.

Jesus is expressing God's desire and intent to go out of His way to call out to and restore those who do not deserve it. This irked the self-righteous Pharisees but was music to the ears of the 'tax collectors and sinners', who were despised and regarded as the lowest of the low.

Unbelievers can clearly be guided by God to achieve His purposes

As has already been established, God is the Lord of all creation, who not only reveals Himself to the wayward and lost but also instructs those who do not know him to accomplish his work.

A classic Old Testament example of an unbeliever clearly being directed to achieve God's purpose is Cyrus, King of Persia, who conquered the Babylonians around 540BC. A couple of years later, he issued a decree allowing the Jews, who had been exiled to Babylon seventy years earlier, to return to their homeland. Initially, as reported in the books of Ezra and Nehemiah, about 50,000 people made the journey.

However, the book of Isaiah makes plain that Cyrus did not take this course of action entirely of his own volition: 'Thus, says the Lord, your Redeemer... who says of Cyrus, "He is my shepherd and he shall fulfil all my purpose"; saying of Jerusalem, "She shall be built", and the temple, "Your foundation shall be laid." Thus, says the Lord to his anointed, to Cyrus, whose right hand I have grasped, to subdue nations before him and to loose the belts of kings, to open doors before him that gates may not be closed: "I will go before you and level the exalted places, ... I will give you the treasures of darkness and the hoards in secret places, that you may know that it is I, the Lord, the God of Israel, who call you by your name. For the sake of my servant Jacob, and Israel my chosen, I call you by your name, I name you, though you do not know me. I am the Lord, and there is no other, besides me there is no God; I equip you, though you do not know me..."' Isaiah 44:28 to Isaiah 45:5

This would suggest that, not only did God direct Cyrus's decision, for the sake of His own people, but also the rise of Cyrus as a conqueror of nations and all his success was God's sovereign work.

Q&A: God's First Overtures

The following questions explore how and when each of us first came to recognise God's communication for ourselves.

1. a. Have you always been aware that God exists and that He is behind the creation or were you formerly either oblivious to or hostile to that notion?

   b. Before you knew anything much about Him, did you think God was interested in you personally?

   c. What kind of personality did you attribute to God before you got to know about Him?

2. When and how did you receive your first inkling of the truth about God?

3. Would you say that God has pursued you – giving you multiple opportunities to appreciate the truth before you responded decisively? If so, what did He do to create and present those opportunities?

4. Has God used or worked through any 'unbelievers' (people whom you were not aware of having a relationship with Him) in order to reveal Himself to you or to impress upon you some aspect of the truth about Himself?

Of those pursuing relationship with God, how many are in the habit of actually listening to Him?

"Why do you call me 'Lord, Lord', and not do what I tell you?"
Luke 6:46

Many may accept the notion of God wanting to deliver messages to us, from time to time, but *how* would you expect it to happen? A majority might be comfortable with such a sense coming either via His written word or someone expounding His written word. Those are the kind of experiences a lot of us have become familiar with, especially if we are used to reading the Bible and/or listening to preaching.

A lesser number might expect Him to speak through a dream or a vision or perhaps the exercise of one of the gifts of the Holy Spirit during a church gathering but we are inherently more suspicious of those mechanisms because we don't understand them quite so well.

And even fewer would expect communication to happen via an entirely non-human agency, such as an audible voice or the visit of an angel.

Leaving the mechanism to one side for a moment, how *often* would you assume God might want to talk to you – on a regular basis or relatively infrequently? A high proportion of people seem not to believe that God wishes to engage with them on a daily basis. Some believe that God stopped speaking at the close of the canon of scripture. A great many think He has bigger and better things to do than to talk to us. The New Testament, on the other hand, repeatedly argues against such beliefs.

It is 'natural' for God to speak to us personally

We looked briefly at John 10 in the Introduction but let's consider it again: Jesus says, 'My sheep hear my voice, and I know them, and they follow me. I give them eternal life, and they will never perish, and no one will snatch them out of my hand.' (Verses 27,28). And again, 'The sheep hear his (the shepherd's) voice, and he calls his own sheep by name and leads them out... and the sheep follow him, for they know his voice. A stranger they will not follow, for they do not know the voice of strangers.' (Verses 3-5). This describes an ongoing relationship of trust, between the believer and Jesus, that involves regular instruction and guidance. The Good Shepherd always works in the best interest of the sheep, leading them to pasture, protecting them from predators and giving them rest.

In Luke 8:21, when told that his family had come to find him,

Jesus says, 'My mother and my brothers are those who hear the word of God and do it.' And, similarly in Luke 11:28, after casting out a demon from a man and being called 'blessed' by someone in the crowd, Jesus says, 'Blessed rather are those who hear the word of God and keep it.' There's a measure of rebuke in both these cases. Jesus is calling people back to the central requirement of a relationship with God, namely to listen and to obey His word.

In Romans 10:17, Paul says, 'So faith comes from hearing, and hearing through the word of Christ.' Hearing what God is saying to us is the prerequisite for faith – there is no surety unless God has said it but, if He has spoken and we have heard Him, we can depend on His word. Isaiah puts it this way; 'As the rain and snow come down from heaven and do not return there but water the earth, making it bring forth and sprout, giving seed to the sower and bread to the eater, so shall my word be that goes out from my mouth; it shall not return to me empty, but it shall accomplish that which I purpose, and shall succeed in the thing for which I sent it.' (Isaiah 55:10,11)

Hebrews 3:7 says, 'Today, if you hear his voice, do not harden your hearts...' And 4:12 says, 'The word of God is living and active, sharper than any two-edged sword, piercing to the division of soul and of spirit, of joints and of marrow, and discerning the thoughts and intentions of the heart. And no creature is hidden from his sight, but all are naked and exposed to the eyes of him to whom we must give account.'

There is always a 'now-ness' and 'up-to-date-ness' about God's word and it's the only thing in the universe that can tell us the truth, on a daily basis, about our real thoughts and intentions. Once we grasp the fact that it does not inconvenience the God of the universe for us to ask His opinion, there should also be a commitment on our part to seek His face about every issue that arises or concerns us.

Q&A: Normal, Everyday Choices

The verses quoted and the examples given above show that God doesn't just want to speak to people on special occasions, He is communicating with His creation on a regular basis. The scriptures also indicate something of His purpose in speaking and introduce the idea of it being both 'normal' and necessary because, otherwise we can't 'have faith' for the outcome.

1. Looking back over the time you have known or at least known about God, have you been aware of His desire to talk to you and, if so, in what ways has that benefited your relationship with Him?

2. Of all the major decisions that you have made in your life (e.g. where to live, which job to take, who to marry [if applicable], which responsibilities to accept and which to decline – in other words all the times you had to make a choice when there were two or more options and the choice had consequences), how often did you know for certain what was the right thing to do? Record two or three examples and explain how you knew.

3. Thinking back through all those choices, how did you decide what to do when you were not at all sure of the right course of action and how did it turn out?

4. Have there been any occasions when you have known the right thing to do but haven't known either how it would turn out or how you would handle the process but you have nevertheless 'had faith for it'? If so, record one or more examples.

The power of God's words (and therefore our words)

"So shall my word be that goes out from my mouth; it shall not return to me empty, but it shall accomplish that which I purpose, and shall succeed in the thing for which I sent it."
Isaiah 55:11

Hearing what God has to say – and obviously believing it and, as necessary, applying it to an opportunity or a problem or a need – can be the difference between something happening and nothing happening; between achieving His specific purpose for us (or for someone else) or not achieving it. To appreciate this principle, we need to look a little closer at 'words' and what happens when they are spoken.

When we speak, we rarely think about the impact that our words will have on those that are listening. We don't often focus on the consequences – i.e. what will happen as a direct result of what we have said. Some of what we say is superficial, even flippant, but some is laden with intent; positive or negative, blessing or curse. We hopefully do people good by some, or even much, of what we say but we tend to be brought up short only when someone, either legitimately or unreasonably, takes offence or when we hear of a tragedy that has resulted from someone's verbal unkindness or incitement.

The Bible has much to say about the power of words, notably in the book of James: 'How vast a forest is set ablaze by a small fire! And that is what the tongue is: a fire! Indeed, among all the parts of the body the tongue represents a world of its own, a world representing the sum-total of wickedness. It defiles the whole body, and catching fire from hell itself, it sets aflame the very driving-wheel of our existence... No human being is capable of subduing the tongue... With the tongue do we offer praise to him who is our Lord and Father; and it is with the tongue that we invoke curses upon our fellow men, who have been created in God's image.' James 3:5-10 (Cassirer, 1989)

Jesus issued a stark warning in Matthew 12:36,37: 'I tell you this: men will be held accountable on the Day of Judgment for every careless word they utter. It is according to the words you have spoken that you will be acquitted. It is according to the words you have spoken that you will be condemned.' The reason He was so direct and forceful was because, after casting out an evil spirit and restoring a blind and dumb man both to sight and speech, He had been openly accused by the Pharisees of consorting with Satan. He was appalled at the truth-twisting and corruption that He saw around Him and knew clearly that (as He would later go on to explain) '...the things that proceed out of the mouth come from the heart, and those (are what) defile the man.' (Matthew 15:18)

The way that both Jesus and James talk about the tongue, above, using words like hell and cursing and wickedness and judgment, is in keeping with the Old Testament warning: 'Be careful what you say and protect your life. A careless talker destroys himself.' Proverbs 13:3 (Good News Translation). We are responsible for what we say and for how we handle (administer) the word God speaks to us.

Our own 'human' words possess power because we have been created in God's image and His words have always possessed extraordinary power. However, whereas our words may come from an unrighteous heart, God's words always issue from a just and gracious heart. Whereas our words may be harmful or counter-productive, God's words always achieve His divine purposes.

So powerful and accurate are God's words that everything of any importance has been initiated by God speaking:

- the Old Testament starts with the 'Spirit of God hovering over the face of the waters' and God bringing the world into being by uttering a series of 'Let there be' proclamations (Genesis 1);
- the New Testament starts with an angel stating to Mary that 'the Spirit of God will come over you, and the power of the Most High will overshadow (hover over) you' and 'you will conceive in your womb and give birth to a son' who will be the 'Son of the Most High' (Luke 1:30-35);
- the Son begins His ministry by invoking God's prophetic word through Isaiah, 'The Spirit of the Lord God is upon me to bring (speak) good news to the poor, ...to proclaim liberty to the captives, ...to proclaim the year of the Lord's favour' (Isaiah 61:1-3);
- the risen and ascended Son gives birth to the Church by declaring to the disciples, 'you will receive power when the Holy Spirit has come upon you, and you will be my witnesses' (Acts 1:8) and ten days later, 'they were all filled with the Holy Spirit and began to speak in tongues as the Spirit gave them utterance...' and 'Peter, standing with the eleven, lifted up his voice and said, "Men of Judea and all who dwell in Jerusalem, let this be known to you..."' (Acts 2:4,14);
- the writer to the Hebrews sums up the operation of the word of

God among those in the Church by saying, 'For the word of God is living and active, sharper than any two-edged sword, piercing to the division of soul and spirit, of joints and marrow, and discerning the thoughts and intentions of the heart.' (Hebrews 4:12);

- the end of all things is heralded, in the Revelation to John, with the words, 'And I heard a loud voice from the throne saying, "Behold the dwelling place of God is with man. He will dwell with them, and they will be His people, and God himself will be with them as their God. He will wipe away every tear from their eyes, and death shall be no more, neither shall there be mourning, nor crying, nor pain any more, for the former things have passed away" And He who was seated on the throne said, "Behold, I am making all things new."'

At every stage, the Spirit of God has been and will be present as agent, with power to bring about the intended result of the word that is spoken. All of God's words are spoken with specific intent – not one is superficial or flippant and none can be discarded. To put it another way, His words express truth and beget actions – when God speaks, something happens.

To support and establish this point, I am going to borrow some words from a wonderful book by Thomas Smail, called 'Reflected Glory':

'The activity of the Spirit is evidenced by the fact that his words and deeds were performed with God-given authority. A typical comment on the early ministry of Jesus is that "they were astonished at his teaching, for his word was with authority" (exousia) (Luke 4:32). So also of his works, "With authority (exousia) he commands the unclean spirits, and they obey him" (Mark 1:27). And the same idea expressed without the use of the word, "And the men marvelled saying, 'What sort of man is this that even winds and see obey him'" (Matthew 8:27). As well as the lives of men, the secrets of the supernatural and the elements of nature are subject to his power.

'In this context the word 'authority' is very strong indeed – it means a God-given right and power to effect that which he commands. His words were characterised not merely by their intellectual validity

and truth-content, but even more by the power that was in him to make happen that which he said. This is the characteristic of the divine word (dabar) in the Old Testament, "And God said, 'Let there be light' and there was light" (Genesis 1:3). The word of Jesus operates in precisely the same way, "He said to the paralytic, 'I say to you, rise, take up your pallet, and go home'. And he rose and immediately took up the pallet and went out before them all; so that they were all amazed and glorified God, saying "we never saw anything like this" (Mark 2:10-12). This visible happening was, in the context of the narrative, the outward sign of the invisible event of the forgiveness of sins which (v5) his word had effected with the same authority.

'Precisely this connection between the authoritative word spoken and the visible event that results from it is evidenced again and again as characteristic of the ministry of the Holy Spirit in the New Testament Church.' (Smail, 1975)

God's word is the only source of motive power in the universe – His words create and they sustain; He builds up or breaks down; He restores and repairs or dismantles and destroys; and on each occasion He declares His intention in words.

We have become used to talking about God's word and His power but rarely do we hear it and see it directly. Thomas Smail goes on to say that the Jewish authorities in Jesus' day were so troubled by *'the present power'* of Jesus' ministry that they sent him to the cross. In other words, they could not handle the real manifestation of the Holy Spirit *doing things* before their very eyes, in direct response to Jesus' words, when all they had known and understood until that point was what Tom calls 'intellectual theory and pious practice'. The threat that He posed both to the status quo and to the religious leaders' carefully constructed power base was too great.

If the Holy Spirit is still intent on bringing into actuality the words of God, let's be careful neither to try and hide behind a wall of safe theological argument nor to assume a standardised course of action but rather give God the opportunity to demonstrate His work. If we want to know His intent for a situation, or His opinion on a matter, or His solution to a problem we would do well to ask Him and then listen to what He has to say. We don't, in ourselves, possess the necessary wisdom or the power to affect issues and people for good. So, if we want to be involved in God's work and, just as importantly, to avoid messing it up, we need to get into the habit of discerning what is His solution, and then passing it on, rather than make up our own or take a formula off the shelf.

Q&A: The power of words

1. Are you aware of the power that your words possess, for good or ill, and the difficulty of staying in control of what you say?

    a. Can you think of any instances when you have witnessed an immediate effect of what you have said?

    b. Have there ever been times when you have asked God to give you a word of instruction or wisdom or comfort for a situation that someone was facing?

    c. If so, did your intervention have a positive effect?

2. Can you recall situations in the Bible, from both Old and New Testaments, when there was an immediate physical and material effect of the words that someone said?

3. In the biblical examples you have highlighted, what kind of situation or difficulty was being experienced at the time and what did God's intervention achieve?

4. Do you think it is legitimate to expect God to speak into the situations and difficulties that you and others around you are facing?

5. If your answer to Q4 is 'Yes', how might that alter the way you view and potentially address those issues?

Our preferred outcomes are not always God's will

"I am God, and there is no other; I am God, and there is none like me, declaring the end from the beginning and from ancient times things not yet done, saying, 'My counsel shall stand, and I will accomplish all my purpose.'"
Isaiah 46:9,10

It is important to establish another principle here – we previously quoted Romans 10:17 (about faith being dependent on the word of Christ) and, although that verse is talking primarily about faith for salvation, it makes clear that believing God must come from hearing what He has to say. You cannot have faith for something until He has spoken about it but, once He has spoken, you can have certainty because, whatever He says, His word is absolutely trustworthy.

In Luke 17 we find Jesus entering a village on the border between Galilee and Samaria and encountering ten men with leprosy. They shout to him and ask Him to have pity on their condition. When you look carefully at the passage, you'll notice that He does not pronounce healing but shouts back that they should go immediately and present themselves to the priests (which you would only do if you were clean from your leprosy). They obey His injunction and, as they go, realise that they've been cleansed. If you had asked them about their preferred outcome, at the point when they started shouting, this would undoubtedly be very close to it.

When one of them turns around and comes back to express his gratitude, Jesus says to him, 'Be on your way, it is your faith that has given you back your health.' (Cassirer, 1989) This man did not have anything on which to attach faith for healing before Jesus appeared in the village. But, having heard Him issue an instruction and having decided to obey that instruction, whilst still in a leprous state, his faith was kindled and he is commended for it.

In Luke 18 we have an encounter between Jesus and the 'rich young ruler' or 'man of influence', who asks Him, 'what must I do to obtain eternal life?' After a short conversation about his having kept the commandments, Jesus says, 'One thing you still lack. Sell everything you have and divide the proceeds among the poor. Then treasure shall be yours, a treasure in heaven. And after that, come and follow me.' The young man cannot accept Jesus' condition and walks away dejected. (Cassirer, 1989)

Jesus had put His finger on the core issue that was keeping this man from embracing the kingdom of God – the issue that, in Jesus' eyes, was every bit as dangerous as leprosy. However, the instruction the man received did not represent his preferred outcome and we infer from the passage that he could not obey the word.

It is not for us to make our own assumptions about the origin of a problem or the timing of a solution or what God should grant as an outcome. To discover His will for a situation or to obtain His help with a problem, we first need to ask Him and then, having asked, do what He tells us, whether His answer is our preferred way forward or not. That means there are a couple of very big questions we must consider:

- Will we seek His face about *everything*, and be ready to accept His judgment on each matter, whether or not we agree with that judgment? and;
- Will we trust God even when it seems as though He has forgotten or abandoned us or when the outcome we desperately want is denied?

It is vital that we read the whole and not just part of the word of God and somehow achieve a balanced set of expectations for the outworking of 'life in Christ', both for ourselves and for those we care about. Too often God is portrayed as someone who will jump to attention if we just pray the right prayer or adopt the right doctrine but God is not like us and His ways are not our ways. Yes, His love is extraordinary, His mercy unfathomable and His grace (as a famous preacher once put it) 'ridiculous'! But, His holiness is absolute and His wisdom beyond measure and He is fashioning us for eternity, not for a comfortable, temporal existence.

As a result, the process of discipling, which is intended to make us more like Jesus, so that we are one day accepted into His presence as 'sons' in full measure, must be rigorous. There will necessarily be ups and downs, highs and lows, times of clear understanding and others of utter bafflement, victories and seeming defeats in our walk with God.

We rarely understand by instinct *what* He wants to do in a particular set of circumstances or *how* He wants to do it and our reflex reactions can often be a long way off the mark. To get some more insight into what we are talking about here, let's look at the period of time covered by just one chapter of the gospel record – Luke 9. This chapter presents a remarkable catalogue of Jesus' interactions with His disciples as they observed Him, learned from Him, asked

Him questions and sought to process the mass of information being presented to them and the new and bewildering experiences that He was taking them through.

We find the disciples got some things right, when they carefully followed the instructions that Jesus gave them, but frequently got other things wrong, whenever they:

- misinterpreted Jesus' intentions or declared their preference for an outcome other than the one He had in mind;
- failed to appreciate that the particular difficulty facing them was actually a test;
- didn't grasp the enormity of what Jesus was saying and, as a result, failed to appreciate the cost required to achieve the outcome;
- misunderstood the strategic importance of the situation and why He had invited them into it;
- got carried away with their own importance or stepped outside the permissions He had given them;
- failed to understand the nature of the kingdom or to see the bigger picture.

Luke 9 begins on a high, with Jesus giving the twelve power and authority over demonic spirits and all diseases and sending them out to proclaim the kingdom of God, with strict instructions on how to behave, all of which they do successfully (verses 1-6). It goes on to chronicle His feeding of the 5000, where the disciples react instinctively to the practical impossibility of meeting the needs of a vast crowd but don't realise that Jesus is testing them. Their advice to Him is to send the people away – His response is, '*You* give them something to eat' (verses 10-17).

Then we have Peter's great confession, 'you are the Christ, God's anointed' – another high but with a slight sting in the tail because it appears that, left to their own devices they will use the information unwisely and they have to be told, in the form of a rebuke, both to keep quiet about what they know and not to think of themselves too highly but to be ready to 'take up my (Jesus's) cross daily' (verses 18-27). This is followed by Jesus taking Peter, James and John up a mountain and being transfigured before them. Despite these three having earlier 'seen' and testified to the truth about Jesus' identity, they cannot cope with His unmasking and fall back on an intensely human set of responses that are inappropriate for the occasion (verses 28-36).

Their return to the other disciples and the crowd is not a happy one – their compatriots have failed to expel a demon and there is much disquiet. Jesus has to step in and we know [from Mark 9:29] that they have completely underestimated the seriousness of the boy's condition and what preparation is required in order to minister to that kind of need. The wonder that grips all those who are watching Jesus at work leads Him to impart solemn instruction to the disciples about their having underestimated the enormity of His mission and what it will take to complete it. He again tells them of the suffering He must go through, lest they focus only on the accomplishments and get carried away with euphoria (verses 37-45).

Luke then records three incidents, one after another, where the disciples demonstrate that they have not yet properly heard what Jesus has been teaching them and, in each case, He has to administer a rebuke:

- Firstly, they engage in an argument among themselves about who is the most important (verses 46-48). Had they been listening when He told them not to think of themselves too highly and to 'take up His cross' in verse 23? Or, is our human nature so insidiously opposed to the ways of God that such lessons need to be repeated a number of times before we 'get it'?
- Secondly, they report that they have forbidden someone, who is not of their number, from casting out demons in the name of Jesus. Jesus, on the other hand, can see a bigger picture and a greater purpose (verses 49-50).
- Thirdly, they are present when a Samaritan village refuses to welcome Jesus and, rather than follow the guidelines that He gave them a little earlier in verse 5 (namely, 'shake off the dust from your feet as a testimony against them'), they are ready to call down fire from heaven to consume the whole lot (verses 51-56)!

We who are pursuing relationship with Jesus are, similarly, being discipled by Him and we are prone to the same mistakes.

We are frequently bewildered by what is going on around us and sometimes overwhelmed by either having to face significant difficulty ourselves or by witnessing the trauma and difficulty of others. Jesus states what is needed, clearly and succinctly, in Luke 9:44: 'Let these (my) words sink into your ears...' The only way for us to 'get it right' is to listen carefully to what He says and to follow His instructions rather than to give in to emotion or instinct or to adopt our own best guess.

We know intuitively, as well as from the clear teaching of the New Testament, that life is not plain sailing; that there will be difficulty and opposition and some suffering along the way; that we are living in a fallen world and that death is an inevitability. Suffering is one of the many things that we are actually 'called to' – 1 Peter 2:21 says, 'For to this you have been called because *Christ also suffered for you, leaving you an example*, so that you might follow in His footsteps.'   And Paul, when setting out for the Philippians his impeccable, personal credentials then declares, 'whatever gain I had, I counted as loss for the sake of Christ. Indeed, I count everything as loss because of the surpassing worth of knowing Christ Jesus my Lord.' He goes on to say, 'For his sake I have suffered the loss of all things and count them as rubbish, in order that I may gain Christ... that I may know him and the power of his resurrection, and *may share his sufferings, becoming like him in his death...*'

Why then, when facing a problem, do many of us automatically assume God is duty bound to lift the problem from us and remove any discomfort we are experiencing? Why do we tend to resort to a formulaic approach to praying – a form of words that is intended, magically, to invoke God's power on our behalf – rather than seek His face with an expectation of hearing Him and then allow Him to direct our prayers? Why also is the cause of a difficulty almost always attributed to 'an enemy', when there are so many examples of God himself testing His people?

Please do not misunderstand me, I wholeheartedly endorse the claim that God heals today and that He intervenes in space and time, to alleviate adverse conditions and relieve the effects of our human weakness, and I know we have an enemy, but it is folly to argue, as some do, that it is God's primary intent *on every occasion* to heal or to remove an obstacle or to cut suffering short.

Unless we consider ourselves to be fashioned from altogether more favourable material than Jesus' disciples and therefore immune from rigorous discipling, we must submit to His methods and those will involve some discomfort. Jesus will test us but He will always have our ultimate good in mind – He won't settle for us being less than we could be. Like a good parent He will instruct, coach and encourage us but He will not remove all adversity from our path – He will allow certain things and even actively make use of them because otherwise how will we grow and mature and gain wisdom? As is set out in James 1:12,13, 'Blessed is the man who remains steadfast under trial, for when he has stood the test he will receive the crown of life, which God has promised to those who love him.'

But neither is Jesus playing a game with us whereby we become unsure what the origin of the difficulty might be – He is trying to teach us the difference between testing (where the associated difficulty is necessary to build character and resilience) and temptation (where the difficulties that ensue are the product of our own weakness and fallenness and are not constructive but damaging to our life and work). As James says immediately following the verse quoted above, 'Let no one say when he is tempted, "I am being tempted by God," for God cannot be tempted with evil, and he himself tempts no one. But each person is tempted when he is lured and enticed by his own desire. The desire when it has conceived gives birth to sin, and sin when it is fully grown brings forth death.' (1: 13-15).

Being discipled builds discernment and the benefit of discernment is being able to appreciate the origin of a difficulty – is this from God or is it from an enemy? What I think the New Testament is urging us towards is learning how to discern something of what He is doing, in each situation we face, and then to pray accordingly. That way, we will more often be praying 'in faith' and in agreement with His thinking and more likely to pick up the nuances of His activity and the subtlety of His Holy Spirit's work.

Picking up those nuances will surely tell us when there is still too little information about an issue to warrant a particular course of action; when we should be engaging in spiritual warfare; when we are under God's judgment or subject to His testing; when we should be 'standing firm' on a promise He has made; when He is present to heal etc.

Q&A: Faith comes only from having heard

1. When you think back through having had to face issues of concern over the years:

   a. You will presumably have been aware of having preferred outcomes but did those affect the way you sought God's intervention?

   b. On the occasions that you took action or intervened in response to an issue did you do so 'instinctively' or did you ask God what the right approach should be in that moment?

   c. Our responses and the actions taken can vary tremendously, depending on mental and spiritual state at the time. Can you recall occasions when you felt some or all of the following: i) confident of a particular outcome; ii) fairly confident but with a measure of uncertainty; iii) 'all at sea'; iv) that you were definitely 'barking up the wrong tree'?

   d. Did God ever surprise you with a different outcome to what you were expecting?

2. If the outcome that we would instinctively prefer when facing a particular situation might not be God's will, how should that alter the way we approach each situation?

3. If you were to take seriously Jesus' punchline ['everyone who comes to me and hears my words and does / does not do them'] from the story about 'building your house on the rock / sand' (Luke 6:46-

49) or His punchline ['My mother and my brothers are those who hear the word of God and do it'] from the occasion when His mother and His brothers came to see Him (Luke 8:19-21), would that change the way you conduct your relationship with Him?

4. How has your faith been affected both by the way you have approached issues of concern in the past and by the way they have turned out?

Communicating with God is a two-way thing

"Thus, the Lord used to speak to Moses face to face, as a man speaks to his friend."
Exodus 33:11

For a relationship to exist means there *has* to be communication of some kind. It's both a necessary component and inevitable by-product of an ongoing human relationship and it is no different with a relationship between God and a human. The communication may start out only one-way – from Him to us – because it was while we were still ignorant of His plan of salvation that 'God... spoke in time past to the fathers by the prophets, [and] has in these last days *spoken to us by His Son*' Hebrews 1:1,2. Furthermore, as we saw in Jesus' parable about 'The Lost Sheep', in Luke 15:4-7, He both pursues us and is delighted to find and re-establish relationship with us. However, God has always intended the communication to be a two-way thing and there is more to its two-way nature than we might have realised.

The activity of the Holy Spirit and Prayer

When we first respond to Jesus' call and trust Him with our lives, He gives us the Holy Spirit, who then constantly witnesses with our spirit that we are now a child of God - Romans 8:14-16. This activity of the Holy Spirit enables us to share something of the Father's heart and His will (for us and for the situations and people around us) and also to sense in our spirit when He is saying something particular to us.

Our ongoing communication with God inevitably involves prayer, in some form, and the nature of prayer is conversation – when we pray, we are looking for that 'one-way' communication to become 'two-way'; we express something heart-felt and we hope for, even expect to receive, a response. But, there are occasions when it feels as though God has not heard us! Why is that?

People have written whole books to try to answer this question – one or two have been helpful but reading some has left me none the wiser afterwards. I suspect my reaction to the latter may not be the author's fault, it probably had more to do with me treating the whole 'answer to prayer' thing too theoretically – at the time, I didn't have an active appreciation of what it meant to 'hear God' for myself and I wasn't confident in discerning what He might or might not have been saying, concerning the issues I was praying about.

If you *do* have some confidence to discern what He might be saying, as you entreat Him, you can do two things that the person who lacks confidence cannot do:

Firstly, you can present a situation to God in prayer and, rather than simply ask Him for your preferred outcome, you can ask Him to tell you what *He* wants to say about it... whatever that might be;

Secondly, you can be content to work with His response and run with whatever He says, no more and no less... however different or 'disconnected' or limited your human spirit may think His response is, compared to your own 'ideal'. In my (albeit limited) experience, if you do that, God quite quickly gives you further insight or 'intelligence' about the situation.

Factors that affect performance and outcomes

In our attempts to pray and to receive responses from God, there are at least 5 factors to take account of:

1. His ways are not our ways – Isaiah 55:8,9 says, 'For my thoughts are not your thoughts, nor are your ways my ways, says the Lord. For as the heavens are higher than the earth, so are my ways higher than your ways, and my thoughts than your thoughts.' We lose sight, especially in times of stress, of just how different our 'fallen' way of thinking is, compared to His righteous and all-knowing way. Nevertheless, He intends that His ways should become ours in increasing measure as we submit to His Holy Spirit and begin to perceive a little of how He views the situations we face. If we only knew some of what is going on in the spiritual realm, I suspect that our prayers would be radically different;

2. Certain obvious things can obstruct our prayers – As those who have placed our faith in Jesus, we know that, unless we are being deliberately disobedient, or asking for something that is contrary to His revealed will or asking with an obviously wrong attitude, He will definitely have heard the prayers we offer – 1John 5:14,15 says, 'And this is the confidence that we have toward Him, that if we ask anything according to His will He hears us'.

   However, there are places in the Old Testament, e.g. Isaiah 1:15 and Jeremiah 11:14, where God expressly warns the people that He will not listen until they repent and do what He has *already told* them to do. Also, Isaiah 58 deals with what God calls 'the false fast' and 'the true fast' i.e. humility, repentance, an absence of wickedness and a sharing of resources with the poor must take the place of seeking our own pleasure, quarrelling and withholding what is due. He explains how transgressions are preventing God from hearing His people's entreaties.

Then, in the New Testament, James 4:3 says, 'You ask and do not receive because you ask wrongly, to spend it on your passions.', and similar messages about prayers being hindered are found in 1Peter 3:7 and 1John 3:21,22. Asking God to make you aware of any transgression and practising an attitude of repentance reverses this state, puts us back in a state of righteousness, by His grace, and gives us assurance of being able to find His ear;

3. <u>We often lack the necessary persistence and patience</u> – If we are not deliberately disobedient but dependent on His grace, He will hear us and, if we believe He is just and His word is true, it behoves us first of all to be persistent - to keep on asking because 'God will give justice to His elect, who cry to Him day and night.' (Luke 18:1-8 – Jesus' parable about the Persistent Widow). Then, secondly, we are bidden to 'have the full assurance of hope until the end, so that we may... be imitators of those who through faith and patience inherit the promises' (Hebrews 6:11,12).

4. <u>We tend to rely on formulae or 'the way we did it last time'</u> – some of us will be familiar with the verses in John 14 where Jesus says this to His disciples; 'Truly, truly I say to you, whoever believes in me will also do the works that I do; and greater works than these will he do, because I am going to the Father. Whatever you ask in my name, this will I do, that the Father may be glorified in the Son.' When we read the 'whatever your ask in my name...' part of this, there is a temptation to assume we will magically get what we ask, as long as our prayer contains the words 'in Jesus name'.

In fact, Jesus is not giving us permission to use a formula when praying. For example, the disciples had to be corrected on many occasions, not least when making assumptions about a particular case, such as in John 9: when confronted by a man who had been born blind, the disciples ask whether it was he or his parents who had sinned for this to have happened. Their question suggests they are ready to address the sin and for that to result in his healing but Jesus has to tell them that they are wrong on both counts.

The disciples' question could have been prompted by Jesus' response to the man at the pool of Bethesda in John 5:14 or His words to the woman caught in adultery in John 8:11 or perhaps by the way he handled the man who was let down through the roof in Luke 5:20 but they were to learn that every situation requires fresh intelligence from the One who heals.

An unfortunate consequence of making assumptions or using a formula is that, if something doesn't happen in response to a person's prayer, very often either the one praying or the one being prayed for is accused of not having enough faith!

When Jesus gave assurance that those who believe in Him would do the same works, He was talking about two things – the fact that His return to the Father meant the Holy Spirit would be sent upon those who believe and also the desire of His Father and Himself to come and set up their 'home' with(in) the believer. It is talking about us forging relationship with Jesus, which in some way mirrors Jesus' own relationship with His Father, and the Holy Spirit leading us into all truth.

We will absolutely see great answers to prayer but the relationship with Jesus is key to that happening, as is our increasing ability to discern what the Holy Spirit is saying and doing, as we speak with Him;

5. There is something properly mysterious about God's communication with us – this harks back to point 1 above, and the gulf between His and our respective ways of looking at things. As we will see later, in a discussion on His innovative means of attracting our attention and on the types of message He issues, He may choose to provide clear and detailed instructions in one case and either limited or no instruction in another! He has His own sovereign reasons for doing this but, although we may not understand His reasons at the time, we do know that He is good. His sovereign decisions about how much to tell us are mysterious but so are the mechanisms He uses to convey that information. He speaks 'spirit

to spirit' but it is always a bit of shock when, having not heard a conventional voice, we find ourselves 'just knowing' something that we previously did not 'know'.

When it comes to praying, we may be in the habit of using words i.e. consciously bringing to God our own and others' needs and specifically asking Him to tell us His will and purpose. But, sometimes we don't have sufficient clarity to be coherent. At those times, we could heed Paul's injunction in 1Corinthians 14 to use the gift of 'tongues' ['...one who speaks in a tongue speaks not to men but to God... he utters mysteries in the Spirit' (verse 2) and 'I want you all to speak in tongues, but even more to prophesy' (verse 5)].

Whether or not that is part of our theology, we may still find ourselves silently rehearsing our longings and yearnings and expressing what is on our hearts without ever resorting to words because, just as God doesn't often speak to us in an audible voice, neither is one necessary from our side. As it says in Romans 8:26, 'Likewise the Spirit helps us in our weakness. For we do not know what to pray for as we ought, but the Spirit intercedes for us with groanings too deep for words.'

In terms of response to our prayers, although God is at liberty to speak something 'out of the blue' (something we were not anticipating that becomes a real 'game-changer' in our lives), much of what He says may be a continuation of an ongoing conversation. By 'conversation', I mean a sequence such as: the Holy Spirit planting truth in us; then acting as witness to our spirit grappling with that truth; us resolving or coming to terms with the truth and then Him responding to what has been going on and presenting an answer or an instruction or a way forward.

Q&A: Listening & Speaking – a Conversation

Assuming the results of your attempts at prayer, like mine, are sometimes clear and explicable and sometimes differ from what you desired, it becomes extremely important that we hear God's responses accurately and grapple with the answers He gives:

1. Are you in the habit of talking to God? Jot down a short and honest summary of your current prayer habits.

2. Do you pray about the big decisions of life and, if so, has the process of coming to a decision typically taken a short time or a longer period?

3. Has there been a recognisable, two-way conversation between you and God during that discovery process – i.e. you asking Him something; Him giving you some guidance; you seeking further understanding (or even arguing with Him!); and Him providing clarification? If so, what are the ways that God has used to speak to you?

4. Do you pray about the day to day decisions – e.g. the setting of priorities; the outcome of encounters with people; specific tasks that have to be undertaken; difficult situations to be faced etc? If so, what are some examples of the times when God has given direction or influenced outcomes?

Confirmation
and Confidence

"If any of you lacks wisdom, let him ask God, who gives generously to all without reproach, and it will be given him. But let him ask in faith..."
James 1:5,6

Seeking wise counsel

When we need direction for our lives or to know how to tackle a particular problem or we are unsure of the right way to proceed, our *first* port of call should not be our church leaders, or a 'mentor' or to seek the advice of a spouse or of friends. As a matter of priority, we should go to God and trust Him to speak to us and, in the end, it is His advice we ought to take.

I have known people who, when they have a problem, are in the habit (as their initial response) of asking one or more other people for their input, rather than asking God. Their tendency is to look to others to make decisions for them and it's a dangerous practice. We are each responsible before God for how we conduct our lives, and as valuable as Church leaders and advisors and friends may be to us, we cannot ultimately rely on what they say or allow their opinions alone to shape what we do.

Input from the wise people in our lives *is* important – it can teach and instruct, support and advise, confirm and encourage or indeed rebuke and redirect – but our primary source of wisdom should be direct communication with God because there is always a possibility that human input may be flawed.

Good advice or the right advice?

Human advisors may mean well and the advice they give may be wise 'in general' but it may also be inappropriate for the trajectory God is taking us on at the time. In Acts 21:10-14, Luke relates a time when Paul is given advice by a prophet called Agabus. The word is a warning about what will happen if he goes to Jerusalem and both Agabus and the others gathered there in Caesarea with him strongly urge him *not* to make the journey. Paul, on the other hand, has already been talking to God and he knows that things will not go well in Jerusalem. In spite of that, he also senses that it is right to go. Agabus' prophetic insight was correct but his conclusion, concerning Paul's action, was incorrect - both he and Paul's other friends wanted to protect him but, in this case, avoidance of danger was not God's will and purpose.

Like Paul, we may receive *good* advice but not the *correct* advice. When it comes to guidance or instruction, God never bypasses the one to whom that guidance or instruction needs to be given and we can depend on him to speak. The role of a wise person, whose counsel we seek, should therefore be to help and encourage us to hear God for ourselves.

Romans 12:1-2 is such a well-known passage that it is possible to gloss over certain parts of what it is saying: 'I appeal to you therefore, brothers, by the mercies of God, to present your bodies as a living sacrifice, holy and acceptable to God, which is your spiritual worship. Do not be conformed to this world, but be transformed by the renewal of your mind, *that by testing you may discern what is the good and acceptable and perfect will of God.*' This is advocating a different way of thinking – something we have to learn by trial and error; something we will gain confidence in as we learn to present ourselves to God and to hear His voice, distinct from all the other voices that clamour for attention.

Experience tells us we will not get an unequivocal answer each time we pray and we will not necessarily know the 'right answer' the first time we sit down to seek God and to contemplate the options. Neither will we always know how to interpret what we think God might be saying to us. There will be times when we need to ask Him for confirmation. There will be times when we know we only have part of the story and will need both patience and determination to keep asking.

We are meant to be discerning people, who (either alone or alongside others) give God a chance to speak, who sense what He may be saying to us and then grapple with it, weighing the options. If we begin to operate in this way, it will not be long before we know that a 'right' conclusion leads to a peaceful resolution – in other words, there is a deep sense of 'rightness' and 'peace' that results from resolving an issue with God; knowing that you have got close to understanding His word to you.

We should not be afraid that to embark on a quest to 'hear God' will put us on a slippery slope to some intense, over-spiritualised and therefore abnormal existence! It is not abnormal, it is biblical and it's of the essence of a day-to-day walk with God.

Q&A: Learning to Discern

Confirmation of the 'rightness' of a course of action is something we can expect God to give. However, we are called upon to learn how to discern wrong from right, good from bad, short-term fix from long-term solution. We are also told to test what we think we may have heard, however 'reliable' we might regard the source – when Paul is writing to the Thessalonians about how to lead a life pleasing to God and how to interpret the times and the seasons, he says, 'Do not quench the Spirit. Do not despise prophecies, but *test everything*; hold fast what is good. Abstain from every form of evil.' 1Thessalonians 5:19-22

1. Can you think of any biblical examples where someone who is told to do something seeks a means of confirmation before going ahead?

2. Can you think of any biblical examples where someone gets instructions from God but, even after receiving confirmations, fails to believe the word and tries to back out?

3. Have you ever had a situation in your life, when:

   a. God has spoken to you directly and you have then received confirmation from another source of what He had said?

   b. Someone has spoken something (e.g. in a sermon or during a conversation) that you believed to be a word from God to you, or someone has deliberately brought something to you and said that it is a word from God, and you have then received confirmation directly from God?

   c. You have received something from another party or you thought you had heard something directly, which you subsequently did *not* act on because, when you tried to test it, you believed it was not an accurate message from God?

God's ways of attracting our attention

"[Jesus prayed] 'Father, glorify your name.' Then a voice came
from heaven: 'I have glorified it, and I will glorify it again.' The
crowd that stood there and heard it said that it had thundered.
Others said, 'An angel has spoken to him.'"
John 12:28,29

We are going to take some time to look at a series of people in the Bible to whom God spoke decisively. The examples fall into three broad categories:

- Interventions by God with no apparent forewarning, which could be seen as Him enlisting the help of one of His servants to bring about His sovereign will in a situation.
- A word from God in direct response to questions asked or petitions made in the normal course of a person's duty or the outworking of their responsibilities.
- The continuation of a conversation that began previously or the outworking of a word which was planted previously in someone's heart and for which they had been awaiting an outcome – in almost all cases, the fulfilment or the next decisive stage in the process involves God taking further initiative in an unforeseen manner.

It's instructive to look at the references in context and to see the circumstances in which communication occurs i.e. *what* happens and *how* the word comes, and then the nature or *intended outcome* of the word spoken – the story is different in each case.

Seventeen of God's creative strategies arranged chronologically

A call to complete a journey that someone else started:

Abram (Genesis 11 & 12) – Abram's father, Terah, had taken the family and begun a journey from Ur to Canaan but had stopped in Haran. Was the reason he couldn't go any further because his son, who, we are told, had previously 'died in the presence of his father... in Ur', was also named 'Haran'? Sometimes, although we have a clear objective, we get stuck because of tragedy or trauma. We are not told why the son was so named but it is possible that Terah had family connections here and named him after the place.

Then, "the Lord said to Abram, 'Go from your country and your kindred and your father's house to the land I will show you. And I will make of you a great nation.'" We are not told *how* God said that to Abram. His call seems to be a renewing of his father's call but it could have been something entirely new – either way, having started the journey from Ur, he knew God was drawing him to a new place. He took 'ownership' of the original decision his father had made to go to Canaan and was willing to obey God's leading, despite (as Hebrews 11 says) 'not knowing where he was going (to settle)' and despite already knowing that Sarai was barren.

Looking at the relative ages of Terah and Abram, as stated in Genesis, it seems that Abram began his pilgrimage some sixty years before his father died, leaving Terah in Haran. If indeed Terah had family connections in the area, he would have been content to be left among them.

A strange occurrence that shakes you out of the normal routine:
Moses (Exodus 3) – Whilst working for his father-in-law, pursuing the life he had had for forty years, Moses was made to turn aside from his normal course by an arresting sight. It turned out to be (the angel of) the Lord speaking to him out of a burning bush. The call of God took a bit of explaining but was essentially the fulfilment of what He had said to Abraham, in his sleep, way back in Genesis 15:13. Moses was going through a normal working day, operating according to habit and out of responsibility. He was not looking for a diversion or a new job and so God needed to do something noteworthy – something sufficiently abnormal for Moses to take notice.

We should also take notice of what it says in Exodus 3:4 – 'When the Lord saw that he [Moses] turned aside to see, God called to him out of the bush, "Moses, Moses!".' This is the God with whom we have to do – He was watching intently to see if Moses would 'take the bait'. He is not aloof and distracted, He is attentive, interested and committed to speaking to us.

An audible voice in the night:
Samuel (1Samuel 3) – The word of the Lord was rare. Eli, the person who should have been hearing God for the people, was corrupt and, both actually and symbolically, was losing his sight. Samuel was just a child – he had been dedicated to God by his mother, in fulfilment of her promise, and would have been weaned by four years old but Josephus puts his likely age, at the time God called him, as eleven. A conversation between God and Eli had been ongoing but Eli had failed to heed the warnings and so God was commissioning another 'seer'. He came and called the boy three times because this was a totally new experience for Samuel and God knew he would not recognise His voice the first time. He then spoke to Samuel in words the child could understand and entrusted to him His word of judgment.

In need of instructions on how to fight a battle:
 Joshua (Joshua 5) – He had taken over from Moses and had led the people of Israel across the Jordan, to begin to occupy the Promised Land. God had already spoken to him clearly on several occasions; giving instruction for the crossing, the setting up of a memorial and the circumcision of all the males born since the nation left Egypt. Now, in Joshua 5, he finds himself near to Jericho, in need of a plan, and 'The Commander of the Army of the Lord' comes to him unannounced. There is some similarity with what happened to Moses at the burning bush – a heavenly visitor and a piece of holy ground where you have to remove your shoes. What is then communicated in detail to Joshua is a unique strategy for overcoming Jericho.

Different instructions for two almost identical situations:
David (2Samuel 5) – Two battles, between Israel and the Philistines, occurred within days, or at most weeks of each other, both in the Valley of Rephaim. David did not receive a heavenly visitor but, on both occasions, we are told that he 'enquired of the Lord'. Although the circumstances of both battles were almost identical and the result of following God's instruction the first time was a decisive victory, David did not fall into the trap of using the same

methodology for the second encounter. God's instruction for the second battle was radically different to the first – as with Joshua, a strategy both unique and un-guessable.

A friend and colleague bringing timely advice:

Nathan to David (2Samuel 12) – After the unlawful affair with Bathsheba, God sent Nathan to David with a message in the form of a parable. There was no guarantee that David would understand and then respond appropriately but, despite his sin, God knew David's heart. David acknowledged his guilt and accepted both the responsibility for and the consequences of his actions. David needed someone to 'hear God' for him and to have the courage to bring the word because his own actions had obscured his judgment and blocked his ears. 'Faithful are the wounds of a friend.' Proverbs 27:6.

Images and word association:

Jeremiah (Jeremiah 1) and Amos (Amos 8) – It was common for God to give visions and pictures of everyday things to the prophets or to show them a common object and then to tell them what that picture or thing was an illustration of. It was also common for God to use 'a play on words' – a word or phrase that sounds like something else or has more than one meaning. In Jeremiah 1, God says, 'Jeremiah, what do you see?' And Jeremiah says, 'I see an almond branch.' Then the Lord says, 'You have seen well, for I am watching over my word to perform it.' The point being that 'of an almond tree' [Heb: sha.Ked] sounds like the Hebrew word for 'am ready / am watching' [Heb: sho.Ked].

Again, in Amos 8 God says, 'Amos, what do you see?' and Amos says, 'A basket of summer fruit.' Then the Lord said to him, 'The end has come upon my people Israel; I will never again pass by them...' The association here is that the Hebrew words for 'the end' [Heb: hak.Ketz] and 'of summer fruit' [Heb: Ka.yitz] sound alike. The Spirit of God somehow attracted the prophet's attention, at a particular time and place, to 'see' something in a way he wouldn't normally see it. God gave that 'something' a significance in the moment and communicated a message through it.

Reading God's Word Pt1 – Understanding what God is saying now:
Daniel and the prophecy of Jeremiah, (Daniel 9:2) – Soon after Daniel and his friends, Shadrach, Meshach and Abednego, and a host of others had been taken to Babylon, Jeremiah had written a letter to the exiles, regarding the length of their captivity.

According to Jeremiah 29:1-23, it was written '…after King Jeconiah and the queen mother, the eunuchs, the officials of Judah and Jerusalem, the craftsmen, and the metal workers had departed from Jerusalem – (whom Nebuchadnezzar had taken into exile from Jerusalem to Babylon)' and it instructed the exiles to, 'Build houses and live in them; plant gardens and eat their produce; …multiply there, and do not decrease. But seek the welfare of the city… for in its welfare you will find your welfare.' Daniel and his friends believed this to be the word of the Lord and so they applied themselves to understanding the Chaldean culture and were rewarded with high office. The letter also stated, 'For thus says the Lord: When seventy years are completed for Babylon, I will visit you and I will fulfil to you my promise and bring you back to this place.'

Many years later, we read in Daniel 9, 'In the first year of Darius, a Mede, who was made king over the realm of the Chaldeans, I Daniel perceived in the books the number of years that, according to the word of the Lord to Jeremiah the prophet, must pass before the end of the desolations of Jerusalem, namely, seventy years' (verses 1,2). Knowing the time was drawing near, Daniel set himself to fast and to pray and to beg mercy from God, that He might fulfil His word.

A Pagan King consulting the history of his Pagan Nation:
Esther and the plot to annihilate the Jews (Esther 3-6) – We looked at this earlier in the book but it bears retelling in this context. Esther, the Jewish girl whose older cousin and guardian Mordechai had introduced her to the court of King Ahasuerus in Susa, was now Queen. However, the king and his senior officials did not know she was Jewish. Later, at the instigation of Haman, who was the most senior official in the kingdom and who hated Mordechai, an edict was written in the name of the King that all Jews were to be killed. Mordechai found out about the plot and persuaded Esther to agree

to help the Jews. So, Esther took her life in her hands, sought the favour of the King and then prepared a banquet to which she invited both the King and Haman. In the meantime, Haman had gallows constructed on which he planned to hang Mordechai.

On the night before Esther's banquet, the King could not sleep. Esther 6:1 says, 'He gave orders that the 'book of memorable deeds', the chronicles (that recorded noble things that people in the kingdom had done), be read to him. And it was found written how Mordechai had told about Bigthana and Teresh, two of the king's eunuchs, who had sought to lay hands on King Ahasuerus.' As a result, the king determined to reward Mordechai for his timely warning and, in the following, breathless sequence of events, Haman's plot unravelled and he was hung on his own gallows.

God is here guiding someone to do His will when that someone would not normally acknowledge Him. His intervention was timed perfectly and He used secular, written material to speak to His chosen servant.

A Sudden, Unexpected Reaction to a piece of news (a heightening of the senses):

Nehemiah hearing of the situation back home in Jerusalem (Nehemiah 1) – Nehemiah, a Jew who had been born in captivity and had never seen his homeland, was going about his daily duties as cup-bearer to King Artaxerxes. All had not been going well back in Jerusalem, even though two substantial parties had previously returned there from Babylonia/Persia (50,000 people under Zerubbabel, 90 years previously, and then about 2000 people under Ezra, 14 years previously).

And then some Jews arrived in Susa, having travelled from Jerusalem, and Nehemiah made a point of asking them for news. They reported that, 'The remnant there in the province... is in great trouble and shame. The wall of Jerusalem is broken down, and its gates are destroyed by fire.' (verse 3).

Their words have a devastating effect on Nehemiah – if he had not realised, up to this point, the degree to which his own heart's desires were tied up with the state of his homeland, he definitely knew it now and verse 4 says, 'As soon as I heard these words I sat down and wept and mourned for days, and I continued fasting and praying before the God of heaven.'

This was not a 'normal' reaction and it took Nehemiah completely by surprise. What he did in response shows that God was speaking to him and had been preparing him for just such an event.

Nehemiah's prayer is recorded in verses 5-11 and it is remarkable not just because of its heart-felt honesty and fervour but also because it shows him, though several generations removed from those who were originally exiled from Judah, to be a student of the Hebrew scriptures and familiar with the ways of God. It was not an outbreak of emotionalism, it was a deep longing for God's purposes to be worked out. He wholly identified himself with the people of Israel, put himself in their position, confessed their sins as though they were his own and, knowing that he would now have to try and do something about the problem himself, called on the God of heaven to grant him favour with the king.

There will be times in our lives when something 'resonates' with us and the degree to which our senses are heightened will be noteworthy. It behoves us on these occasions always to bring the reaction to God. Like Nehemiah, we might already have sensed that it is He who has spoken to us but, then again, we might not immediately know that. It is important for us to discern the origin of what's happened – is it just me or might He be trying to say something.

Reading God's Word Pt2 – Understanding what God has said previously:

Ezra and the Returned Exiles (Nehemiah 8) – After the massive project to rebuild the walls of Jerusalem, all the people gathered to listen to the Law being read. Ezra the Scribe and thirteen other leaders stood on a raised wooden platform to read and were aided by a host of others, including Nehemiah, 'on the ground', to assist the people to understand what was read. They said to the people, '"This day is holy to the Lord your God; do not mourn or weep." For all the people wept as they heard the words of the Law. Then they said to them, "Go your way. Eat the fat and drink sweet wine and send portions to anyone who has nothing ready, for this day is holy to our Lord. And do not be grieved, for the joy of the Lord is your strength." So, the Levites calmed the people, saying, "Be quiet for this day is holy, do not be grieved." And all the people went their way to eat and drink and to send portions and to make great rejoicing, because they had understood the words that were declared to them.' (verses 9-12).

God's word affected those who were listening – conviction of the truth came through hearing – and that effect had to be 'managed'. How important it is that, whenever God speaks, there are those who listen and understand and act accordingly.

A visit from an angel:

Mary (Luke 1) – After 400 years of near silence there was an explosion of spiritual activity prior to and after Jesus was born. We read in various places of angels bringing messages to people but few responded as humbly and graciously as Mary. God sent Gabriel first to Zechariah and then to Mary, a very ordinary young person living in a very ordinary place, and the word changed her life forever. Mary asked Gabriel an eminently sensible question, not unlike the one that Zechariah had asked, but hers was not accompanied by unbelief.

Dreams and warnings:

Joseph (Matthew 1&2) – On four separate occasions we are told that God came to Joseph in a dream to give him warnings and instructions. Joseph was not the only person to experience this means of communication – the Wise Men are another example. Elsewhere in the Bible there are many occasions where God uses dreams to impart information, e.g. with Joseph's namesake in Genesis – very often these are prophetic in nature and proper understanding requires an interpretation to be given.

A sense that life is not complete until a particular something has happened:
Simeon & Anna (Luke 2) – Both were righteous and devout, given to worship and prayer and the word of God had come to each separately, concerning waiting for 'the consolation of Israel' and 'the redemption of Jerusalem'. Remarkably, at the moment of Jesus' dedication, they both 'drew near' and recognised Him. Both were personally fulfilled by the meeting and both not only imparted a blessing on the family but witnessed to Jesus' mission.

An unexpected observation and a compulsion to investigate it further:
The Wise Men (Matthew 2) – These learned men observed something strange and significant in the course of their studies and, interestingly, interpreted it correctly. I would love to know how they did that and what the process involved – maybe one day I'll have the chance to ask them – but the inference is that God so arranged the clues that those 'who had the eyes to see' would recognise them. Their findings were such that they felt compelled to follow up and literally to seek confirmation. Their preparation, their commitment and generosity are an object lesson in hearing and following a call from God. Also pertinent to our understanding of the principles of following a call from God is the fact that the Bible does not indicate these Wise Men followed the star all the way to Jerusalem. They saw it 'when it rose' and they knew that what they had seen concerned 'He who has been born king of the Jews'.

So, travelling 'blind', they went all the way to Jerusalem, where that King was most likely to be, and caused a stir by asking, 'Where is he?'. They didn't know about Bethlehem because they didn't have access to the words of the Jewish prophets until, that is, Herod summoned a conference, called them in and told them the answer. At that point, the star appeared again and guided them. There are times when we know that God has spoken but He may give just enough information to test whether we are willing to take Him at His word. If we are willing to go as far as we are able, He will then provide the next clue.

We also see this principle of diligent investigation described in 1Peter 1:10-12; 'Concerning this salvation, the prophets who prophesied about the grace that was to be yours *searched and inquired carefully,* inquiring what person or time the Spirit of Christ in them was indicating when he predicted the sufferings of Christ and the subsequent glories. *It was revealed to them* that they were serving not themselves but you, in the things that have now been announced.... things into which angels long to look.'

A vision, whilst praying, in which God challenges a foundational belief:

Peter (Acts 10) – Without this vision, of a sheet containing a variety of animals and birds, both 'clean' and 'unclean', received on the roof of a house in Joppa whilst waiting for lunch to be prepared, Peter would not have understood God's commitment to giving the Holy Spirit to the Gentiles. It is difficult to overstate the degree to which this notion was anathema to the Jews. It was an issue on which God had to make an unequivocal statement and then back it up with a clear demonstration at the house of Cornelius, a Roman centurion – 'While Peter was still speaking, the Holy Spirit fell on all who heard the word. And the believers from among the circumcised who had come with Peter were amazed, because the gift of the Holy Spirit was poured out even on the Gentiles.' (verse 45).

The heart being stirred to be involved / to participate in something:

This final category is not part of the chronology above – it gives several examples of God's intervention in a person's day to day walk, where He invades their consciousness for a particular purpose...

- Every man whose 'heart stirred him' or whose 'spirit moved him' (Exodus 35:21; 36:2] – when God gave instructions for the construction of the Tabernacle, a call went out for craftsmen and the indication is that many responded, at least some having to learn new skills in order to be used on the project;
- The Lord stirred the spirit of Cyrus [2Chronicles 36; Ezra 1; Isaiah 44] – a pagan ruler who is referred to, by the God of the Israelites, as 'my shepherd (who)... shall fulfil all my purpose'

(Isaiah 44:28]. Cyrus acknowledged that the Lord had given him power and had charged him with the responsibility of 'building Him a house at Jerusalem' (Ezra 1:2-4) and he duly issued a decree, after seventy years of exile had elapsed, allowing the Jews to return to their homeland;

- 'Everyone whose spirit God had stirred to go up to rebuild the house of the Lord that is in Jerusalem' (Ezra 1:5) – this the response to Cyrus' decree.

The methods used by God in biblical times are still valid now

"For I the Lord do not change; therefore you, O children of Jacob, are not consumed... Return to me, and I will return to you, says the Lord of hosts... Bring the full tithe into the storehouse... and put me to the test, says the Lord of hosts, if I will not open the windows of heaven for you and pour down for you a blessing until there is no more need."
Malachi 3:6-10

In Biblical times, God took ordinary men and women and accomplished extraordinary things with them and through them. He is the same God now as He was then and His ways of attracting our attention today are not going to be too dissimilar (in principle) to those described above.

I have experienced a number of them – there have not been any angelic visits, as far as I know, and I cannot swear to having heard an audible voice (although the instruction was so clear on a couple of occasions, it was like there had been a voice) but I regularly experience some of the less dramatic.

For example: a picture whilst praying; an unexpected observation; a sense that something needs to happen; a dream; a particular interpretation or association or instruction while reading God's word; a timely intervention from a friend. I have also known Him speak to me on several occasions through secular music lyrics – once, a little embarrassingly, at a music festival where I stood among hundreds of people, with tears streaming down my face, as a famous blues artist did his thing about ten metres away.

Q&A: It's Time to get Serious about Listening

God's desire is to give us messages of instruction, inspiration, encouragement, reassurance, strategy, rebuke or consolation or whatever is on His agenda.

1. When was the last time you had an experience similar to one of the 17 mechanisms or principles described? What happened?

2. How many of the mechanisms or principles described can you say have been part of your experience? Think through them and try to recall something similar from your own life – it doesn't have to be some big event, it can be small and still be significant.

   It is not always easy to have past events called to mind when you need them – pray that the Holy Spirit will prompt you over the next hours and days and commit to writing down a reminder as and when something comes to mind.

3. Do you regularly pray for God to attract your attention so that He can speak to you? If not, why not?

So, God has somehow captured your attention... then what?

"Now Elijah the Tishbite... said to Ahab, 'As the Lord, the God of Israel, lives, before whom I stand, there shall be neither dew nor rain these years, except by my word'."
1Kings 17:1

"After many days the word of the Lord came to Elijah, in the third year, saying, 'Go, show yourself to Ahab, and I will send rain upon the earth'."
1Kings 18:1

Having captured someone's attention, God will usually deliver a message, providing either information that was not in the public domain up to that point or additional information to support or clarify something that had been spoken about before.

The purpose is always to reassure or to inform but, as has already been suggested, it could also be to encourage, to motivate, to educate, to commission, to rebuke etc. and it is surprising how often a word from God, because it is communicated spirit to spirit, can accomplish several of those things at the same time.

However, what He says, at a particular point in time, will not necessarily be all that the recipient might want to know. As my Grannie used to say, it might make things seem 'as clear as day or as clear as mud'! It is then a question of whether we are faithful to what He has said – no more, no less – or whether we ignore the word (because we think it inadequate) or, possibly, extrapolate it beyond what has been said and so overstep the mark.

His messages usually fall into one of four categories

Conceptual and general, not concrete and specific – Sometimes the message deliberately lacks completeness and it is necessary to 'go with what you know'. For example, it is said of Abraham, in Hebrews 11:8, that 'by faith he was called to go out to a place that he was to receive as an inheritance. And he went out, not knowing where he was going.' So, he knew he had to go and he knew the direction of travel but he didn't know the end point.

Then there was the boy Samuel, to whom God said in 1Samuel 3:11, 'Behold, I'm about to do a thing in Israel at which the ears of everyone who hears it will tingle.' He then tells him *why* he's going to do it but not what or when or how. At the end of the New Testament, we have the Revelation to John. It sets out in detail what God intends to do but it doesn't specify how or when.

Providing only part of the story – Sometimes God gives someone a part of the story or a clear sense about something He is going to do but it lacks the punchline and requires interpretation. Sometimes He deliberately sets us a riddle or a puzzle or a challenge. In each case, the incomplete information requires people to inquire further, to seek clues and to make observations, or to wait for further information that will give the mandate to act.

Not wishing to repeat arguments set out previously, take a look back at several of 'God's ways of attracting our attention', where He withheld one or more of the *what* or *why* or *where* or *how* or *when* e.g:

- Simeon – who had a good idea of the *what* and *why* and *where* but not the *how* or the *when*;
- The Wise Men – who had a description but didn't know the origin of the *what*, knew *when* and roughly *where* but then had to ask about exactly where;
- The prophets Amos and Jeremiah – who were initially only given something that sounded like the *what*.

There are many more such examples that will present themselves as you read the scriptures.

Detailed and Clear but with a hidden test – This is the kind of message where you think you understand what you have to do but then realise there is a danger of being presumptuous and you must stay absolutely focused in order to get it right. It can resemble the case where you only get part of the story but, instead of being patient until God communicates the rest, there is a need to act and to trust that God will ensure the right outcome. The best example is in the life of Samuel, the prophet.

King Saul had several chances to show that he could follow God's instructions but he failed spectacularly and Samuel had to say to him, in 1Samuel 15:23, 'Because you have rejected the word of the Lord, he has also rejected you from being king.' Then, in 1Samuel 16, the Lord comes to Samuel and tells him to fill his anointing horn with oil, go to Jesse the Bethlehemite, and anoint one of Jesse's sons as the next king. Samuel and God concoct a ruse together, about his needing to visit Bethlehem to conduct a sacrifice, so that Saul's suspicions will not be aroused, and Samuel duly goes to do the honours. So far so good.

The hidden test in this, for Samuel, is that Jesse has eight sons and God has not told him which of the eight to anoint. They are brought before Samuel in order of age and when Eliab, the first and oldest, is presented there is a dialogue between Samuel and God in which God coaches him as to how to make the decision: '[Samuel] looked on Eliab and thought, "Surely the Lord's anointed is before Him." But the Lord said to Samuel, "Do not look on his appearance or on the height of his stature, because I have rejected him. For the Lord sees not as man sees: man looks on the outward appearance, but the Lord looks on the heart."' So, Samuel passes on Eliab and then on each of the next six. Thus, we come to the crucial part of the test – there are no other sons available and Samuel, to his credit, does not panic! He asks Jesse, 'Are all your sons here?' To which Jesse replies, 'There remains yet the youngest, but he is keeping the sheep' (verse 11).

They wait for the youngest to be summoned and, when he arrives, God says clearly to Samuel, 'Arise, anoint him, for this is he' (verse 12). Isn't God strange – why didn't He divulge the key piece of information sooner?

Detailed and Clear – God sometimes sets out precisely what he wants, what it should look like and who needs to do it. For example, the building of the Ark in Genesis 6; the building of the Ark of the Covenant, the Tabernacle and the Priest's Garments in Exodus 25-28; the defeat of Jericho in Joshua 6; the building of Solomon's Temple in 2 Samuel 7, 1 Chronicles 28-29 & 1 Kings 5-7. In each case the plans were extremely detailed and those tasked with carrying them out were required to achieve unprecedented levels of quality and craftsmanship.

Moving into the New Testament, the Angel Gabriel, when he came to Mary in Luke 1, explained clearly what God was about to do and then answered her questions. In Acts 8:26-40, Philip was given precise instructions by an angel about where he was required to go and, when he got there, he met the Ethiopian eunuch. In Acts 9:10-19, Ananias was given precise instructions in a vision about where to find Saul of Tarsus and what to do when he got there. Then, in Acts 11:27-

30, Agabus prophesied about the timing and extent of a famine which was about to happen and the church was warned to gather and to send relief to those who would be affected.

Q&A: If You were God, What Would You Do?

My categorisation of God's messages may not be the best but, if you think it is at least reasonable, let's use it to think through our preferences and how God has taught us important lessons:

1. If you found yourself in God's position, like Jim Carrey in 'Bruce Almighty', with people petitioning you from all sides (and assuming you were not pushed for time), which of the above four kinds of message would you tend to use and why?

2. If you would not choose to use a certain kind of message, why do you think God persists in doing so?

3. As we have already intimated, God's communication with us might be intended for any or all of information, reassurance, encouragement, motivation, education, commissioning or rebuke. So, try to think of several important lessons that you've learned over the course of your life – can you recall what types of message God used in each case?

God often withholds explanation and may even deliberately conceal the truth

"The secret things belong to the Lord our God, but the things that are revealed belong to us and to our children forever, that we may do all the words of this law."
Deuteronomy 29:29

If I were God, I would err on the side of providing a full and complete explanation whenever I wanted something done. I would probably overcompensate on the information given, to leave no room for error or excuse. However, there are many biblical examples of God deliberately holding back on detail when He gives someone a message or hiding the meaning of His words from His hearers.

God reveals only as much as He considers necessary
Abraham and Samuel – when Abraham upped sticks and left Haran, he was doing the only thing he had been told to do and when the boy Samuel told Eli what God had said to him in the night, he told him everything he'd heard. These guys were not acting on limited information due to being hard of hearing – they were responding to as much as God had revealed at the time and they trusted that God would reveal more when the time was right.

Samuel (again) – when the prophet Samuel came to anoint the next king of Israel, why did God withhold a key piece of information? Two reasons come to mind:
- Firstly, He wanted Samuel, just as He wants us, to remain dependent on Him throughout the task at hand. He wants it to be a partnership because teamwork is so important to Him – and He knew that it was a priceless opportunity to coach Samuel and improve his skills of discernment.
- Secondly, we are prone to making decisions based on outward appearance or for other 'superficial' reasons. Note that, when Samuel saw the first son, Eliab, he said to himself, 'surely this is the Lord's anointed'. Was he thinking back to Saul, whose presence must initially have made an impact on him? Recall that 1 Samuel 9:2 says, '[Kish] had a son whose name was Saul, a handsome young man. There was not a man among the people of Israel more handsome than he. From his shoulders upward he was taller than any of the people.'

To digress slightly for a moment; for those of us prone to fear of missing out, there is encouragement to be taken from the selection process – David, Jesse's youngest son, was not present when Samuel came to call but that did not mean he missed God's purpose. God has things for each of us to do and we can be sure that He will not overlook us, despite circumstance or logistics or others seeming to occupy the prime positions.

The Disciples – when, in the words of Luke 9:43-45, 'everyone was full of wonder at all the things which Jesus was accomplishing', Jesus said to His disciples, 'There are certain words of mine which you must keep in your minds once and for all: "The Son of Man is destined to be betrayed and to be given up into the power of men."' You'd think that the disciples would take that to heart and ponder it but we go on to read, 'They did not, however, comprehend what they were told; indeed, it was being kept hidden from them, so that they should fail to grasp its meaning.' (Cassirer, 1989). These were the people whom Jesus had determined should know the truth and so we can only surmise that His words, on this occasion, were either to await their time or were too devastating for the disciples to deal with right then.

A noble and generous heart, childlike faith and something worrying about parables

Why does God sometimes seem to leave so much to chance, when He could be more explicit in His detail, and why sometimes does He deliberately withhold understanding?

It isn't only to do with His timing or our learning processes, it also speaks to the fundamental difference between the person who trusts God and is committed to operating 'by faith' and the person who has no real interest in a relationship with Him.

Where the latter is concerned, it actually doesn't matter how much detail is communicated, they will not believe. We have a clear example of this in the story of the Rich Man and Lazarus, in Luke 16 – they both died and the rich man, having cared nothing for Lazarus, is pictured in Hades, in torment. His request to Abraham was that he send Lazarus to warn his five brothers so that they would repent and would not join him in the place of torment. Abraham is clear; 'if they do not hear Moses and the Prophets, neither will they be convinced if someone should rise from the dead' (verse 31).

As to the deliberate concealing of truth, both Matthew and Luke record 'The Parable of the Sower' and follow it with a discourse on the purpose of parables. In both gospels Jesus draws a distinction between His disciples and the crowd, saying in Luke 8:10, 'As regards yourselves (the disciples), you have been granted the privilege of knowing the very secrets of God's kingdom, while the rest have to be spoken to by way of parables. And the point of it all is that, while looking, they should yet see nothing, and while listening, they should yet understand nothing.' (Cassirer, 1989)

There is intent in this verse, to withhold from some people what is given freely to others, and it is slightly disturbing to those of us who had assumed the parables were always intended to illustrate truths or principles i.e. to simplify and to clarify meaning. Whilst the parables do in fact accomplish that, Jesus makes clear in other places that truth can only be understood by divine revelation – 'No one can come to me (or turn towards me) unless the Father who sent me draws him.' (John 6:44). Paul concurs that humans cannot understand God's truth by natural means – 'The natural person does not accept the things of the Spirit of God, for they are folly to him, and he is not able to understand them because they are spiritually discerned.' (1Corinthians 2:14).

Although we are all invited and all of us *can* come to a knowledge of the truth, the divine prerogative and gracious will of the Father is '*to hide things* from the wise and understanding and *to reveal them* to little children'. Furthermore, all truth was handed over to Jesus, by His Father, and 'no one knows the Son except the Father, and no one knows the Father except the Son *and anyone to whom the Son chooses to reveal him.*' (Matthew 11:25-27).

Jesus communicated very cleverly and deliberately throughout the time of His ministry – not only did He say vitally important things to His close friends which He intended them not to understand until a later date, but He told parables to large crowds in such a way that the truth would actually be unclear to those with no real interest in repentance and faith but lead to revelation for those committed to pursuing Him and being 'discipled' by Him.

So, what qualities do we need in order to maximise our chances of really hearing what He has got to say? The best starting point is

Jesus' description of the 'good soil' into which the sower sowed his seed; 'those who bring a good and generous heart to the hearing of the word, who hold fast to it and, by virtue of their power of endurance, yield a rich harvest' (Cassirer, 1989). Secondly, as we saw in Matthew 11, the Father reveals things to 'little children' – Jesus then says in Luke 18, 'I am telling you this in solemn truth: he who does not accept the kingdom of God in the way in which a child would, will never find entry into it.' (Cassirer, 1989). Then thirdly, recall what Luke says in chapter 18:1, '[Jesus] told them a parable to the effect that they ought always to pray and to lose heart...' There will need to be tenacity to keep on asking and patience in case we only get a partial answer or alternatively an answer that we are not equipped to understand at that time.

Q&A: It's all about.......... timing

1. Can you recall any occasions when God gave you a message but held back on detail which, in retrospect, might have been very useful? From your vantage point today, do you have clues as to why He did that?

2. If He does that again, as He surely will...

   a. Do you feel better able to deal with it than last time? In what ways can you stay alert and ready to hear Him?

   b. How might you plan to work with information that lacks a 'punchline'?

3. Have there been times when you have come to understand or appreciate something and you know it has taken a long time for you finally to grasp it?

   a. Are you able to recall an occasion when you *thought* you understood something but now you definitely *know* you do i.e. it turns out you previously only had a partial understanding but now God has brought much greater clarity to you?

   b. Knowing yourself as you do, are there strategies that you can adopt in order to pursue a proper understanding, whilst managing to remain patient?

The art of mishearing God's word, or even missing it altogether

"When I spoke to you persistently, you did not listen, and when I called you, you did not answer..."
Jeremiah 7:13

Faith does not come naturally and most people's hearing is impaired
Unfortunately, not only does faith *not* come naturally to us, we are beset by blockages to our understanding of God's ways and habitually think in ways that are contrary to God's heart. There seems to be plenty of Biblical evidence that we can be anywhere on the (negative) spectrum ranging from completely deaf to His voice (perhaps due to rebellion / hardness of heart or unbelief or self-absorption), through to barely able to hear (due to dullness of senses), on to being able to hear but still unresponsive.

For example:
- Isaiah 65:2,12 (re-quoted by Paul in Romans 10:21) – "I have stretched out My hands all day long to a rebellious people, who walk in a way that is not good, according to their own thoughts; A people who provoke Me to anger continually to My face... When I called, you did not answer; When I spoke, you did not hear, but did evil before My eyes, and chose that in which I do not delight."
- Isaiah 43 – '...(I) called you by name, you are mine... Bring out the people who are blind, yet have eyes, who are deaf, yet have ears!
- Zechariah 7:11 – '...But they refused to pay attention and turned a stubborn shoulder and stopped their ears that they might not hear...'
- Matthew 13:15 – Jesus says of the generation to whom he was speaking, that the prophecy of Isaiah has been fulfilled: 'You will indeed hear but never understand, and you will indeed see but never perceive. For this people's heart has grown dull, and with their ears they can barely hear, and their eyes they have closed, lest they should see with their eyes and hear with their ears and understand with their heart and turn, and I would heal them.'
- Hebrews 3:7,8 – 'as the Holy Spirit says, "Today, if you hear his voice, do not harden your hearts as in the rebellion..."' Hearing and not responding is a consciously wilful act, slightly different to not hearing at all and therefore not responding. The former is bad but the latter may be worse – a habit of ignoring Him can result in total deafness.

Identity issues may be compounding the problem

Because the greatest commandment is 'love the Lord your God with all your heart and with all your soul and with all your mind' and because the second greatest commandment is 'love your neighbour as yourself' (Matthew 22:36-39), the word of God to us must, at some level, be a challenge to 'self'. Therefore, the way that we view ourselves will have an impact on our understanding of (or colour our interpretation of) the word that God speaks to us and hence, we need to think briefly about the nature of identity.

The question of personal identity is a sensitive subject – people fiercely defend who they believe themselves to be and, consequently, what they believe are their rights. Some are happy with, or even proud of, who they are, whereas others feel ashamed of or disappointed in who they are.

Most definitions of personality and identity suggest that they are 'bio-socially determined', in other words both are genetically pre-defined and socially reshaped. Psychologists suggest that self-identity is the combination of qualities, beliefs, personality, looks and/or expressions that make a person. It is further said that personal identity allows an individual to appear unique through a specific combination of personality characteristics, abilities, interests, physical attributes and biography. The Cambridge English Dictionary defines identity as, 'who a person is, or the qualities of a person or group that make them different from other people'.

It is then suggested that interpersonal identity development comes about through an individual questioning and examining various personality elements such as ideas, beliefs and behaviours. The actions and thoughts of others create social influences that change an individual. This process would allow for someone's identity to evolve over the course of one's life.

The appearance of words like 'unique' and 'different' in the definitions given above is a relief because reading some sociological studies might lead you to believe that all our key characteristics are determined by social influences. Our secular society would essentially have us believe that a person, starting from their genetically pre-defined position, becomes who they are largely through their own efforts and the influence of those around them.

The biblical picture, however, is somewhat different – God is presented as the author of life and the agent of creation; He sets the standards, rescues the fallen, redeems the lost and forgives the repentant; He reveals himself as Father, restores hope and gives purpose. Those who embrace His fatherhood, He can mould, change, develop and sanctify, until, 'we who have been saved are presented blameless before the presence of His glory with great joy', Jude 24. How different is that to the haphazard and chancy outcomes presented by secular society?

Although there may be things about us that are genetically pre-defined and although we may have been heavily influenced and shaped by family and the society around us, looking at identity from a biblical standpoint means that genetics, family and society are not the things that define us.

Additionally, although one person may not have had the privileges or opportunities that another has enjoyed and although he/she may have been prevented from taking chances due to ill health or lack of available resource, looking at identity from a biblical standpoint means that privilege, health and wealth are not limiting factors in who or what they are able to be.

We come to appreciate our true identity – that which is shaped by the God who made us and who deliberately gave us a set of unique characteristics – by revelation. When we put our trust in Jesus Christ, the resulting dynamic relationship is intended to reveal not just who we were always intended to be but also the things He wants us to do. However, our ability to hear God's instruction might be impeded by the view we hold of ourselves:

- We can have too high an opinion and be taken up with our own importance, as we saw in a previous section when the Disciples of Jesus fell to discussing among themselves who was the most important (Luke 9: 46-48). The fact that this happened quite soon after Jesus had been telling them not to think of themselves too highly and to 'take up His cross' (Luke 9:23), confirms that our human nature is dangerously prone to this way of thinking.
- We may, alternatively, have too low an opinion and think we have less value than those around us. Here it is helpful to quote a little medley of verses:

- To remind us that God does have a plan for each one – 'For we are His workmanship, created in Christ Jesus for good works, which God prepared beforehand, that we should walk in them.' Ephesians 2:10
- To reassure us that we are loved – 'Neither height nor depth, nor anything else in all creation, will be able to separate us from the love of God in Christ Jesus our Lord.' Romans 8:39
- To redirect our gaze from self (which can accomplish nothing), to the Lord (who is able to accomplish all things) – 'Trust in the Lord with all your heart, and do not lean on your own understanding. In all your ways acknowledge Him, and He will make straight your paths.' Proverbs 3:5,6

It is also helpful to consider what behaviours and thought patterns might be blocking our appreciation of what God wants to say because to be forewarned is to be forearmed. I have made a list of suggestions, on the next page, as to some of the states of mind that are likely to interfere with our ability to hear, but it is in no sense definitive.

You may find it instructive to stop reading at this point, to put the book to one side and compile your own list, drawing on what you know of your own habits and ways of thinking, before you read my attempt.

Blockages to hearing and understanding what God has to say

Here is my list – it is fairly short because the intention is not to labour the point but to give a few clues as to where, down through the years, I might have tripped up!

- If we don't believe that God speaks to people today or will speak in a way that we can understand, we will tend not to seek Him, or will automatically screen out what He says.

- If we surround ourselves with 'noise' and are rarely quiet, it will not be easy to discern the voice of God amid the clamour. If we do not come aside to think and to pray and if we do not ask for Him to speak, we are unlikely to hear anything.

- If we look for someone else to hear God for us and take no personal responsibility for hearing for ourselves – this can extend to deferring to the pulpit, failing to test whatever we think has been said, looking for some word that we 'like' (and ignoring the ones we don't like) etc. – we will never develop the necessary senses.

- If we focus on our own abilities and are desperate for our own glory (to make a name for ourselves rather than defend and promote God's name) or if we are driving forward to bring our carefully constructed plans to fruition, we will not be looking out for God's purposes or be interested in carrying out His business and hence be in danger of either ignoring His promptings or of never accomplishing something lasting.

- If we are unsure of our own abilities, unaware that God has deliberately made us unique and reticent to put ourselves forward, we may not have understood that the least of us can be caught up in God's purposes and consequently, when He prompts, we will probably argue against Him.

- If God seems to be saying something to us that is in keeping with our dreams and visions and aspirations, we may dismiss His word because a) we have been conditioned to believe that He would never give us something enjoyable to do and/ or b) we don't realise that those dreams are there because He has put them in us. He values our uniqueness, hence His attempts to ensure that the God-given aspects of our identity don't die of neglect.

- If we fail to grasp that our ways are not God's ways, both in the hearing and the doing, and that the word we 'hear' needs constantly to be weighed and tested, we will probably wander off in the wrong direction.

- If we do not have some concrete evidence that at least one of the times, when we thought we had heard God, it was *actually* God, we may develop a habit of discounting all the other times we think we've heard Him. But, if we receive that confirmation of having been right, even if it's only once, we'll start looking at all the other times in a different (and more positive) light.

- If we are consciously or unconsciously living with a sense of failure we are less likely to expect God to be interested in us. As a result, we will probably not be as quick to seek His face and more likely to side-step His initiatives to engage us.

- If we are living in disobedience and/or harbouring unforgiveness, those are obvious obstacles to harmonious and productive communication with God. Also, we may find that a disproportionate amount of His communication with us will be about the need to deal with those issues as a priority.

We tend to compensate for our own limitations, rather than take God's word at face value

God's word needs to be taken seriously and obeyed but we are a fallen people – we do not always deal honestly, we do not see clearly and we do not hear perfectly. As was quoted at the beginning of the workbook - Paul says in 1Corinthians 13, when talking about love, 'For now we see in a mirror dimly, but then face to face. Now I know in part, then I shall know fully, even as I have been fully known.' And as Jeremiah reports in Jeremiah 17:9, when discussing the sin of Judah, 'The heart is deceitful above all things, and desperately sick; who can understand it?'

So, let us be careful because, as has already been argued, we may be tempted not to ask God's advice at all, preferring to apply a formula or to employ the solution that worked on a previous occasion. And even when we do ask and then hear God speak, we are likely to try to compensate for our limitations. For example:

- We will tend to hear what we want to hear and be deaf to what we don't want to hear;
- We will sometimes put our own spin on what we think we've heard, possibly in order to make ourselves look better and possibly to make the story seem more acceptable;
- If we hear something that isn't complete we will be tempted to extrapolate using our own brand of logic and then to proceed accordingly.

These and many more dangers await those who listen for God's word but, despite knowing all about our weakness and capriciousness, God loves us and is still committed to speaking to us. His patience is very great and, if we will submit to His ways, He will disciple us until we begin to resemble His Son.

Q&A: Inhibitions and Limitations

1. What sort of beliefs about God (who He is, what He is like etc.) or belief systems (theology, worldview etc.) might limit our ability to hear His voice?

2. What lifestyles or daily practices are likely to inhibit our hearing?

3. What self-image or identity issues are you aware of that make it more difficult for you to hear Him?

4. How can past failures when trying to hear God's voice (e.g. disappointments we live with, misunderstandings, our wrong assumptions or impetuousness, our unbelief) stand in the way of future success?

Take time to document how God has spoken to you and what He said

"Thus, speaks the Lord God of Israel, saying: 'Write in a book for yourself all the words that I have spoken to you'."
Jeremiah 30:2

We began by asking whether or not you feel comfortable with the idea of God speaking and, if so, whether you are familiar with the process or wary and unsure about it. It is to be hoped that, if you felt uncomfortable and wary at the outset, some of what you have found in this workbook and some of the thought processes it has led you through might have alleviated those negative feelings.

Record your past experience

Whatever your current state of mind, the message of the Bible is that God does speak and that He wants to find ways of communicating with you. It is beneficial to think back systematically, through your life, and to recall the various ways in which you have come to an understanding of the truth. The Holy Spirit is the one who leads us into all truth and so, if you have come to understand something, He has found a way somehow to get through to you, whether or not you have been conscious of the process.

Record your future progress

Having charted the successes and failures so far in your life, it will be beneficial, as the final Question above suggests, to make at least brief notes of what happens from now on. Doing so will of course make future exercises of recall that much simpler but it will also show whether you are making progress.

By progress, I mean becoming more confident at recognising His voice; coming to decisions with more surety; having God attract your attention by a range of different (and possibly new) means. The object of the exercise is not to cross things off a bucket list of communication methods but to achieve a sense of ease in talking with God, not unlike Him walking with Adam and Eve in the garden in the cool of the day.

Q&A: Thinking Back and Looking Forward

In terms of past experience, you will already have noted several relevant examples, in response to previous Qs, and those are still valid as answers to these questions. The idea here is that you work those into a chronology and slot in further examples as and when they come to mind. It is sometimes helpful to divide your life into decades (teens, 20s, 30s, 40s etc.):

1. Thinking back, can you recall any instances where you:

    • Came to an unshakeable understanding of something you knew to be true (maybe by reading the Bible or from listening to a talk or by meditating on a verse);

    • Had a conviction about your own sin and sought to resolve it with God;

    • Sensed clear guidance as to what you should do – either to resolve a dilemma or to show you which course to take;

    • Received advice that you just knew was God's wisdom for a specific situation;

    • Prayed and had a sense of what God wanted to say to someone in need – especially where you followed through and either prayed with that person or spoke the word;

    • Got the distinct impression that God was telling you something but, because it sounded unusual, you were initially unsure. However, whether or not you acted on it, you subsequently found out that it was Him and He was right?

Let God jog your memory and then make brief notes of any times or experiences that come to mind.

2. When you have a few such instances listed, consider the following factors in each case, to see if you can shed more light on the process:

- What was the mechanism (the occasion or activity, the order of events);

- How did the word come to you (a voice, another person talking, a dream, an image, words written out in your mind, a quiet conviction, a slow dawning, a sudden realisation);

- Were you sure and certain or was it vague;

- How did you test it (waited for confirmation from e.g. the Bible or another event, sought someone's wise counsel, 'put out a fleece', just went ahead);

- Did something in particular convince you that it was God speaking;

- What was the outcome?

3. Can you recall times when you either got it wrong (i.e. you think you heard God incorrectly) or did hear correctly but ignored God's voice?

In each case that comes to mind, think through the same set of factors listed above at Q2. Ask God what was the problem in each instance and see if He enlightens you about where the error occurred, so that you can try to avoid it happening again.

At this point, honesty is vital because we often get things wrong through inexperience or emotion or deeply held desires or a sense of injustice or ignorance about what God's word actually says or false confidence or a host of other factors getting in the way.

Discerning God's voice, from all the other voices that clamour for attention, is difficult and demands both practice and persistence. Timothy was brought to the Lord and discipled by Paul and he became a minister in the church in Ephesus. Not many of us have a set of responsibilities the same as his and whilst Paul is not specifically addressing Timothy's hearing of God's word, the principles of needing to practice and to be persistent are the same in our case – look at Paul's injunction in 1Tim 4:11-15.

4. How might you plan to move on from past failure and current weakness and become successful at hearing?

a. Can you be specific about the things that inhibit your appreciation of what God is trying to say to you and commit to praying earnestly about them?

b. Are there one or two people, who are trustworthy and loyal and wise, to whom you can confide? Would they support your initiative in prayer?

c. Over what timeframe do you want to see a marked improvement and how will you record your progress?

A Parting Injunction

God's objective is that we learn to enjoy His company and He has set in motion a process by which those 'in Christ' are led, as individuals, by degrees, from our unholy state to maturity. He has prudently arranged to impart grace to us each step of the way, so that we can complete the journey and not miss out on any part of what He intends us to be. He knows there will be ups and downs but He has plenty of grace to see us through.

So, should we be worried? No, instead we ought to be excited that the God of the universe wants to communicate with us. He is saying, 'Take my yoke upon you, and learn from me, for I am gentle and lowly in heart, and you will find rest for your souls.' (Matthew 11:29). He is promising to give us instruction and to allow us to call on Him whenever we need to. So, let's have a go at listening.

Bibliography

Cassirer, Heinz W. 1989. *God's New Covenant - A New Testament Translation.* Grand Rapids, Michigan : William B. Eerdmans Publishing Company, 1989. 0 8028 3673 9.

Smail, Thomas. 1975. *Reflected Glory.* London : Hodder and Stoughton, 1975. 0 340 20290 4.

Lightning Source UK Ltd.
Milton Keynes UK
UKHW032042200721
387486UK00006B/197